AA

walking in

Snowdonia
& North Wales

First published 2008

Produced by AA Publishing
© Automobile Association Developments Limited 2008

Published by AA Publishing (a trading name of Automobile Association Developments Limited, whose registered office is Fanum House, Basing View, Basingstoke, Hampshire RG21 4EA; registered number 1878835)

Visit the AA Publishing website at www.theAA.com/travel

 This product includes mapping data licensed from Ordnance Survey® with the permission of the Controller of Her Majesty's Stationery Office. © Crown copyright 2008. All rights reserved. Licence number 100021153

ISBN-13: 978-0-7495-5873-4

A CIP catalogue record for this book is available from the British Library.

The contents of this book are believed correct at the time of printing. Nevertheless, the publishers cannot be held responsible for any errors or omissions or for changes in the details given in this book or for the consequences of any reliance on the information it provides. This does not affect your statutory rights. We have tried to ensure accuracy in this book, but things do change and we would be grateful if readers would advise us of any inaccuracies they may encounter.

We have taken all reasonable steps to ensure that these walks are safe and achievable by walkers with a realistic level of fitness. However, all outdoor activities involve a degree of risk and the publishers accept no responsibility for any injuries caused to readers whilst following these walks. For more advice on walking safely see page 112.

Some of these routes may appear in other AA walks books.

Researched and written by John Gillham
Field checked and updated 2007 by Dennis Kelsall and Jon Sparks

Managing Editor: David Popey
Senior Editor: Sue Lambert
Layout and Design: Tracey Butler
Image Manipulation and Internal Repro: Michael Moody
Series Design: Liz Baldin at Bookwork Creative Associates for AA Publishing
Cartography provided by the Mapping Services Department of AA Publishing

A03624

Repro by Keenes Group, Andover
Printed by Leo Paper Group in China

PAGES 2–3: *Llynau Mymbyr near Capel Curig, Snowdonia National Park*
RIGHT: *A view of the river Afon Glaslyn in Beddgelert*
PAGE 6: *Beaumaris Castle on Anglesey*

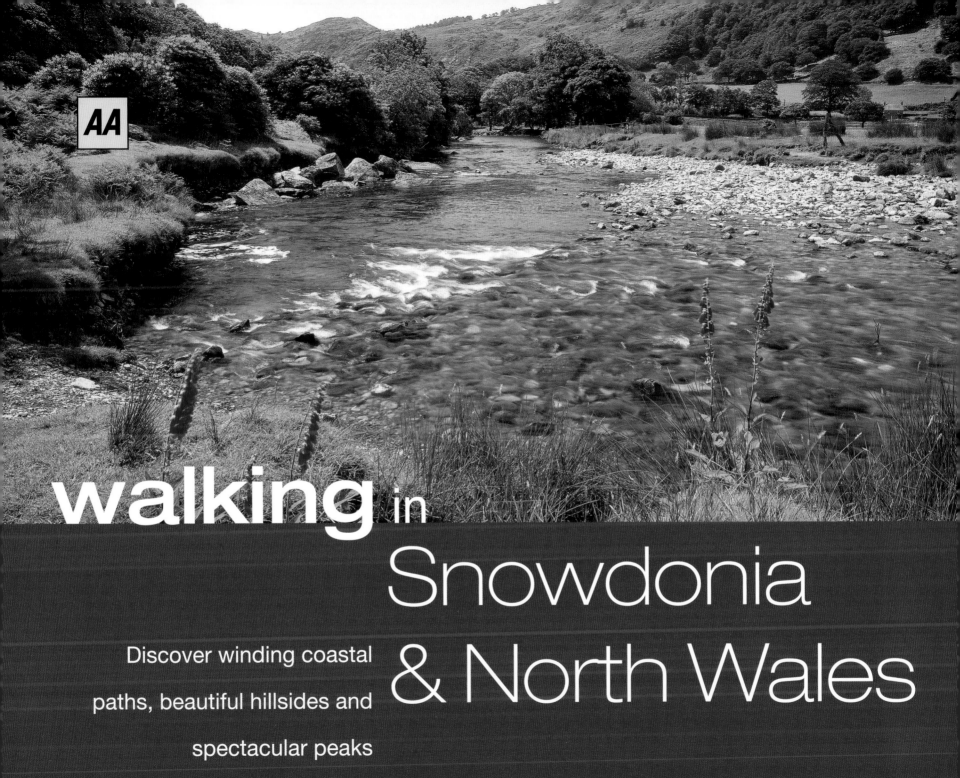

AA

walking in
Snowdonia
& North Wales

Discover winding coastal
paths, beautiful hillsides and

spectacular peaks

Contents

This superb selection of walks introduces the themes and characters that define the beautiful landscape of Snowdonia and North Wales.

Introducing Snowdonia & North Wales

For some, Wales is God's Country. Once you turn your back on the plains of Cheshire and Shropshire, the landscape becomes enticingly hilly, then mountainous. Welsh rivers are boisterous rivers, coursing down from the mountains in white water dashes. Welsh valleys are steep-sided and winding, with secrets around every bend. There are great castles on the coast and great temples of rock in the heartlands of Snowdonia. Having eulogised about it, we should tell you what, for the purposes of this book, the term North Wales means.

Clwyd is the northern gateway to Wales. The old county is green and pleasant, rich farming country with pastures reaching high up hillsides, dotted with whitewashed farmhouses. Valleys like the Tanat and Ceiriog, little known today, have inspired poets for centuries. No one could call Llangollen undiscovered, it's downright busy on most summer weekends, but Llangollen is sited in the midst of north east Wales' finest countryside. The Dee is equally impressive, flowing in great horseshoe meanderings amid the bracken-clad heather hills, the woods and the fields. A walk here can take you up to a hilltop castle, down to an old abbey and ease you along a canal tow path as peaceful as Llangollen is bustling.

The Conwy river separates Clwyd from Snowdonia: the soft greens from the hard grey rock. And the town of Conwy sounds the fanfare for change, with its magnificent town walls and its fairy-tale castle, framed by the great Carneddau mountains. As the walks venture into the Carneddau's expansive area of high whaleback ridges and long uninhabited valleys you will discover the ancient settlements where Iron and Bronze Age tribes lived, and through which Roman soldiers marched. The historical theme continues on the Isle of Anglesey, where it's the coastal walking that appeals.

To the south of the Carneddau, Snowdonia's mountains become even more spectacular with the Glyderau and Snowdon peaks. The Glyderau boast jagged crests with colossal buttresses, the most imposing of these being Tryfan, an almost two-dimensional wedge of rock that towers over Ogwen and its lake.

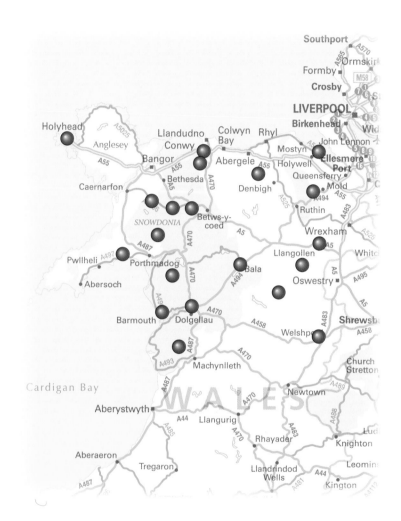

A book of Welsh walks must include a climb to the highest peak, Snowdon. In this book we have tried to be a bit different, choosing to combine the seldom-trod Eilio ridge for the ascent, with the easy gradients of the popular Llanberis path for the descent. It's a long route, but very rewarding. The Snowdonian mountains make a last stand at Cadair Idris, with its ice-scooped corries, arêtes and tarns. If Snowdon is king, then Cadair is crown prince. From the summit you look south to the biscuit-coloured hills of central Wales. Known as the Elenydd or Green Desert, they lack the shape to appeal to the casual walker but for those who take the time to discover them, the Elenydd can be rewarding. You will tread in the footsteps of Owain Glyndwr, come upon little-known waterfalls and crag-strewn mountainsides, and drink from crystal streams. You will have discovered the beating heart of this land of Wales.

map legend

--→--	Walk Route	▓▓	Built-up Area
1	Route Waypoint	▓▓	Woodland Area
- - - -	Adjoining Path	🚻	Toilet
＼ｌ／	Viewpoint	🅿	Car Park
•	Place of Interest	⊞	Picnic Area
⌂	Steep Section	)(	Bridge

using this book

Information Panels

An information panel for each walk shows its relative difficulty, the distance and total amount of ascent. An indication of the gradients you will encounter is shown by the rating ▲▲▲▲ (no steep slopes) to ▲▲▲▲ (several very steep slopes). The minimum time suggested for the walk is for reasonably fit walkers and doesn't allow for stops.

Suggested Maps

Each walk has a suggested Ordnance Survey Explorer map.

Start Points

The start of each walk is given as a six-figure grid reference prefixed by two letters indicating which 100-km square of the National Grid it refers to. You'll find more information on grid references on most Ordnance Survey maps.

Dogs

We have tried to give dog owners useful advice about the dog friendliness of each walk. Please respect other countryside users. Keep your dog under control, especially around livestock, and obey local bylaws and other dog-related notices.

Car Parking

Many of the car parks suggested are public, but occasionally you may find you have to park on the roadside or in a lay-by. Please be considerate when you leave your car, ensuring that access roads or gates are not blocked and that other vehicles can pass safely.

Maps

Each walk in this book is accompanied by a map based on Ordnance Survey information. The scale of these maps varies from walk to walk.

PAGE 10-11: The Snowdon Mountain Railway snakes through the landscape, with Moel Cynghorion and Moel Eilio in the background

The last stop before Ireland, rugged
and rocky Holy Island offers some
of the best walking in Anglesey.

Around Holyhead Mountain

ABOVE: St Cybi's Church was founded
in the 6th century and received
a full restoration in the 19th century.
LEFT: Sailing boats moored at Holyhead Marina

Anglesey's flat and when you motor along the fast and busy A55 to Holyhead the flat fields flashing by the car window confirm the fact. It comes as a surprise then, that when you leave the main road and pass Trearddur Bay, the green fields turn to rugged heathland that rises to a rocky hillside. The locals and the mapmakers call it Holyhead Mountain, and it matters little that it rises to a mere 722ft (220m) above the waves, because this mountain rises steep and craggy and looks out across those waves to Ireland.

Breeding Grounds

The path from the car park heads straight for a white castellated building known as Ellin's Tower. This former summerhouse is now an RSPB seabird centre. The surrounding area is a breeding ground for puffins, guillemots, razorbills and the rare mountain chough: a closed-circuit video camera shows live pictures of these birds. Outside you can look across to the little island of South Stack, with its lighthouse perched on high cliffs. Although the cliff scenery is stunning, a stark, stone shelter and the microwave dishes of a BT station spoil the early scenes, but they're soon left behind as you head to that rocky 'mountain'.

Across the Heath

In this area the footpath traverses splendid maritime heath dominated by ling, bell heather and stunted western gorse. The rare spotted rock rose also grows here. It looks a little like the common rock rose but has red spots on its yellow petals. The footpath eventually climbs over the shoulder of a ridge connecting the summit and North Stack. You'll see a direct path heading for the summit when you reach this ridge. It's a bit of a scramble in places, but worth doing if you're fit and there are no young children in your party. Otherwise, the best route for the more sedate rambler is to head along the ridge towards North Stack.

North Stack

After a short climb there's a big drop down a zig-zag path to reach a rocky knoll with a splendid view down to North Stack, another tiny island. On the mainland, adjacent, there's a Fog Signal Station warning of the more treacherous waters.

The Boats to Ireland

Now the walk cuts across more heath along the north-east side of Holyhead Mountain. From here you'll be looking over Holyhead town and its huge harbour. Once a small fishing village, Holyhead came to prominence after the Act of Union 1821, when its convenient position for travel to Ireland made it the ideal choice for shipping routes. The big ferries and 'cats' will be a feature of this last leg, for you'll surely see at least one glide out of the bay.

PAGE 14-15: South Stack lighthouse on Holy Island, near Holyhead; it is still fully working and tours are available
LEFT: Looking down over South Stack Lighthouse and coastline

walk information

➤ **DISTANCE**	5 miles (8km)
➤ **MINIMUM TIME**	3hrs
➤ **ASCENT/GRADIENT**	1,230ft (375m) ▲▲▲
➤ **LEVEL OF DIFFICULTY**	🚶🚶🚶
➤ **PATHS**	Well-maintained paths and tracks
➤ **LANDSCAPE**	Heathland, coastal cliffs and rocky hills, 2 stiles
➤ **SUGGESTED MAPS**	OS Explorer 262 Anglesey West
➤ **START/FINISH**	Grid reference: SH 210818
➤ **DOG FRIENDLINESS**	Dogs should be on lead at all times
➤ **PARKING**	RSPB car park
➤ **PUBLIC TOILETS**	Just up road from car park

walk directions

1 Take the path for the RSPB centre at Ellin's Tower, a small white castellated building, then climb along the path back to the road which should be followed along to its end.

2 If you're not visiting the South Stack Lighthouse, climb right on a path passing a stone shelter. The path detours right to round the BT aerials and dishes. At a crossroads go left, heading back to the coast, then take

the left fork. Ignore the next left, a dead end path and continue following waymarks over the north shoulder of Holyhead Mountain.

3 Ignore paths leading off right to the summit, but keep left on a good path heading north towards North Stack.

4 After passing through a grassy walled enclosure the path descends in zig-zags down some steep slopes. Joining a track follow it left to a rocky platform, where the Fog Signal Station and the island of North Stack come into full view. Retrace your steps back up the zig-zags and towards Holyhead Mountain.

5 At a junction below the summit path, turn sharp left across the heath. Go right at its end, contouring the eastern side of the mountain. Keep right at a fork and then ignore another summit path from the right. Beyond the mountain, take a right fork as the path comes to a wall. Follow the path downhill towards rough pastureland.

6 Go down a grassy walled track before turning right along another, similar one. This soon becomes a rough path traversing more heathland, now to the south of Holyhead Mountain.

7 Where a waymarked path is later signed off left, bear right below craggy cliffs towards the relay station. Go left at the far end but just before meeting your outward route, swing left again on another path past radio masts. Approaching a service track, bear left again on to a tarmac path. Continue with it over a stile beside a gate, emerging at the end on to the road opposite the café.

8 Turn left along the road to return to the car park.

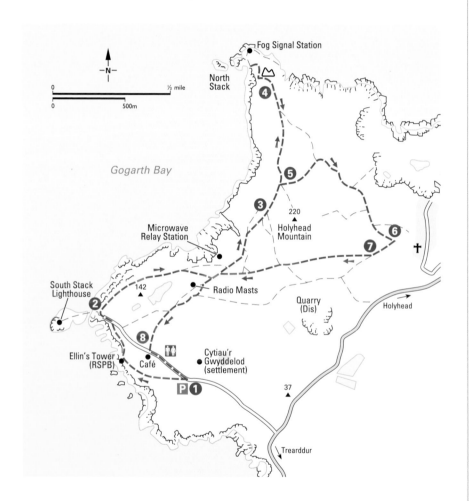

A walk through one of the prettiest woods in Wales, to a high mountain pass.

Pass of the Two Stones

Most people speed by on the A55 dual carriageway without giving Llanfairfechan a second thought or glance. The little Victorian seaside resort beneath the quarry-carved mountain of Penmaenmawr has been forsaken for the castles of Caernarfon and the coastline of Anglesey.

ABOVE: The enchanting woodland of Llanfairfechan
LEFT: Standing stones make a dramatic addition to the landscape

Nant-y-Coed

Llanfairfechan has a secret valley, a beautiful avenue to the big Carneddau mountains. Nant-y-Coed is that valley and Llanfair's early visitors knew it well. In the 1900s it was part of the Newry Estate owned by a Mr Massey. Massey leased the valley to local businessman John Rowland Jones who charged visitors for entry. In 1924, after the sale of the estate, the local council purchased Nant-y-Coed to maintain it for recreational purposes.

A tourist poster described Nant-y-Coed as 'the loveliest sylvan rock and river scenery in Wales', and so it is today. A little path, shaded by deciduous woodland of alder, ash, oak and sycamore, is flanked by the Afon Llanfairfechan, which tumbles over mossy rocks. If the sun's shining, its rays will flicker through the canopy and play games with the water, as will the dipper, who can often be seen scudding across the surface before diving in headlong in search of an insect or two. The bouldery river banks are lined with ferns and wild flowers. In spring the bluebell and wild garlic are predominant, but look out for the star-like white blooms of the wood anemone, also the wood sorrel, a low creeping plant with delicate five- petalled white flowers tinged with lilac.

On to the Moors

As you leave the woods behind and enter what the Welsh called Ffridd, you can see why conservationist John Muir referred to sheep as woolly locusts, for the plant life has been severely diminished by their grazing. Few flowers, except the little yellow tormentil, remain. As you gain height, gorse and bracken have infested much of the pasture, while the odd rowan survives, with wind-warped boughs.

By the time you're at the pass Bwlch y Ddeufaen (pass of the two stones) you're into typical Carneddau moor, where sphagnum moss, cotton grass and rushes fill the marshy areas and heather and bilberry cloak the drier rockier areas. It's a more sombre world, one where the quarrelling ravens and buzzards have replaced the colourful little redstarts and pied flycatchers of the woodland. After following the Roman road along these high moors the route returns to that other world, down the side of Garreg Fawr, where you can see the coastal sands and the Isle of Anglesey, and still further into that sylvan river valley.

walk directions

1 Go through the gate beyond the car park and follow the stony path through the woods of Nant-y-Coed by the stream. Take the more prominent left fork up past the pond, then cross the stream using stepping stones. More stepping stones are used to cross a side stream before climbing to a second car park.

2 A signpost points the way up the valley and you cross a footbridge by a ford to continue. Keep a sharp eye open for stone waymarks, which guide you through a complex series of criss-crossing tracks.

3 The path enters open moorland, still with occasional slate waymarks. Finally, ignore a waymark that points right where the track continues straight ahead. When the path degenerates the direct line is close to steeper rocky slopes on the left. Aim for the col between Foel Lwyd and Drosgl, a point where three lines of pylons straddle the fells.

4 At Bwlch y Ddeufaen a faint path arcs right, parallel to the wall, to join the Roman road. Turn right along the track.

5 At a crossroads of tracks, turn right along the one signposted 'Llanfairfechan' joining the waymarked course of the North Wales Path over Garreg Fawr. After the first grassy summit the path veers left to rake down the west side of the hill to a wall.

walk information

➤ **DISTANCE**	5 miles (8km)
➤ **MINIMUM TIME**	3hrs
➤ **ASCENT/GRADIENT**	1,214ft (370m) ▲▲▲
➤ **LEVEL OF DIFFICULTY**	🚶🚶🚶
➤ **PATHS**	Woodland, field and moorland paths, cart tracks, 5 stiles
➤ **LANDSCAPE**	Woodland, high pasture and moorland
➤ **SUGGESTED MAPS**	OS Explorer OL17 Snowdon
➤ **START/FINISH**	Grid reference: SH 694739
➤ **DOG FRIENDLINESS**	Dogs should be on lead, except on high ridges
➤ **PARKING**	Small car park on Newry Drive, Nant-y-pandy, Llanfairfechan
➤ **PUBLIC TOILETS**	None en route

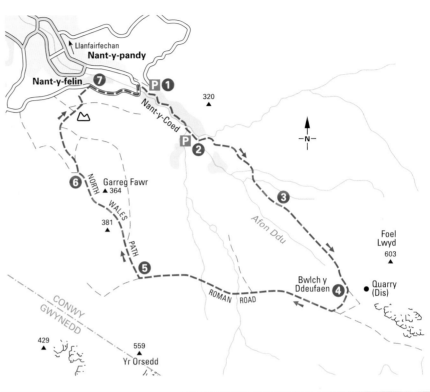

6 Take the waymarked right-hand fork rather than the track following the wall down left. Ignore a narrow path forking right. The main track then threads right and descends steeply through pastures overlooking Nant-y-Coed. Turn left down a little enclosed ginnel to the road.

7 Turn right along the road, which rises then descends to a bridge over the Afon Llanfairfechan. At the other side take the narrow lane back to the car park.

RIGHT: The prehistoric stone circle of Penmaenmawr

Explore the countryside and coastal haunts of the last Liberal Prime Minister.

In the Country of Lloyd George

ABOVE: The 19th-century Church of St John the Baptist stands on the banks of the River Dwyfor in Llanystumdwy
LEFT: Criccieth town nestles close to the base of Cricieth Castle, Gwynedd

David Lloyd George (1863–1945) came from quite modest beginnings in Llanystumdwy. This village on the banks of the Dwyfor is separated from the coast by half a mile (800m) of fields and coastal marshes. When you're barely out of the car park, you'll pass Highgate, his boyhood home, and the Lloyd George Museum. In the woods at the start of the walk you will come across the grave and a memorial to this last Liberal Prime Minister of Great Britain. It's a spot where he loved to sit.

Controversial Life

That Lloyd George was a great man is not in dispute, but his life was not without controversy. Although he was one of the early pioneers of the Welfare State and led Britain to eventual victory in World War One, he was also linked with several dubious private moneymaking deals and gained a, perhaps unfair, reputation for allowing peerages to be awarded to wealthy political benefactors. A flamboyant, larger-than-life man Lloyd George just did not fit in with his rather stuffy Edwardian contemporaries. He is reputed to have been a womaniser, and at one time he had a wife in Criccieth and a mistress, his parliamentary secretary, whom he later married, in London.

Leaving things historical for a while, the walk through the woodland by the Dwyfor riverside is as good as woodland walking gets. The Dwyfor's crystal clear waters chatter to the rocks below and in spring the forest floor is carpeted with primroses, bluebells, garlic and wood anemones. So far we've been heading away from Criccieth and the coast, but soon the route takes us back across fields into Criccieth, a town with history in two episodes.

The Great Castle

Criccieth Castle stands on a huge volcanic crag that juts out into Tremadog Bay. It's synonymous with Edward I's 'iron ring' but, unlike the others, there was already a Welsh castle on the spot – Edward only had to annexe and enlarge it. The twin-towered gatehouse is believed to have been built by Llewelyn the Great, around 1240, some 40 years before Edward took it off him. Yet it was a Welshman who was responsible for the castle's downfall! In 1404 Owain Glyndwr captured it, then burnt it to the ground.

Victorian Expansion

Despite its one-time strategic importance, Criccieth stayed a small fishing port until the Victorians penchant for sun and sand saw it grow to today's proportions. You'll pass the rows of Victorian terraces on the way to the rugged coastal path which takes you by the sand and pebble beach back to the Dwyfor and David Lloyd George's village.

walk directions

1 Turn right out of the car park and go through Llanystumdwy village, past the museum to the bridge over the Afon Dwyfor. Turn right along the lane, then follow the footpath on the left past the memorial and down to the wooded river banks.

2 After 1.5 miles (2.4km) the path turns right, then goes under a stone archway to meet a tarred drive. Turn left along this, carry on to the B4411 and turn right.

3 After about 500yds (457m), turn right down an enclosed drive. As another drive merges from the left, turn half left along a path shaded by rhododendrons. After a few paces, go though the kissing gate, then cross the field guided by a fence on the left. Through another kissing gate the path veers half right, following a fence which is now on the right.

4 Beyond another gate the now sketchy route cuts diagonally (south-east) across two fields to rejoin the B4411, a mile (1.6km) or so north of Criccieth. Follow the B4411 into town. Keep straight on at the crossroads, and bear left after the level crossing to reach the promenade.

5 Follow the coast road past the castle and continue until it turns firmly inland. From here, tide permitting, simply follow the coast path or walk along the sands. Otherwise, follow the road to a bridleway on the left. Go past Muriau and then to the right of Ty Cerrig. Cross a track and a field

PAGE 24-25: Criccieth castle stands high above the Victorian terraces
LEFT: The twin beaches of Criccieth face south and are overlooked from beyond by rising mountains

then turn right on a green track, nearly to the railway. Head left, back to the coast east of Ynysgain Fawr. Follow the coast path west through coastal grasslands and gorse scrub to the estuary of the Dwyfor and some crumbled concrete sea defences.

6 At a metal kissing gate, waymarks point inland. Follow these, with the fence on your right. The route becomes a farm track that cuts under the railway and passes through the yard of Aberkin farm before reaching the main road.

7 Cross the main road with care and go through the gate on the opposite side. A short path leads to an unsurfaced lane, which in turn leads to the village centre. Turn right for the car park.

walk information

➤ **DISTANCE**	6 miles (9.7km)
➤ **MINIMUM TIME**	4hrs
➤ **ASCENT/GRADIENT**	300ft (91m)
➤ **LEVEL OF DIFFICULTY**	
➤ **PATHS**	Generally well-defined paths and tracks, 4 stiles
➤ **LANDSCAPE**	Riverside woodland, fields, town streets, coastline
➤ **SUGGESTED MAPS**	OS Explorer 254 Lleyn Peninsula East
➤ **START/FINISH**	Grid reference: SH 476383
➤ **DOG FRIENDLINESS**	Dogs can run free in riverside woods and on coast
➤ **PARKING**	Large car park at east end of village
➤ **PUBLIC TOILETS**	Near museum at Llanystumdwy and at Criccieth
➤ **NOTE**	Small section of coast path engulfed by highest tides. Make sure you know times of tides before setting off

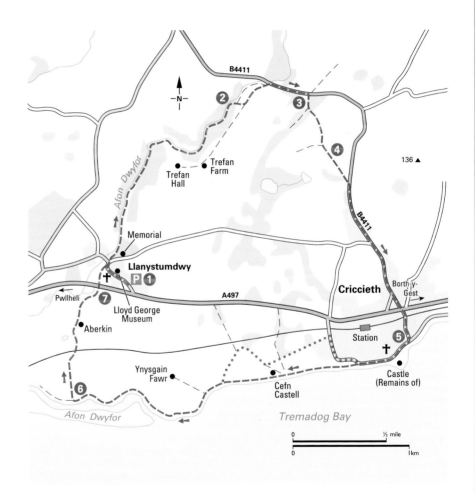

Conwy's magnificent castle lies at the foot of the Carneddau, but up there in the foothills there's a fort, an outpost of the Celtic era.

Conwy: Castle High and Castle Low

ABOVE: The 13th-century Conwy Castle's eight grey-stone towers stand overlooking Conwy
LEFT: Telford's Suspension Bridge stretches dramatically away from Conwy Castle

Conwy is special. Approaching from Llandudno Junction, three fine bridges (including Thomas Telford's magnificent suspension bridge of 1822) cross the estuary beneath the mighty castle, allowing the road and the railway into this medieval World Heritage Site. The fortress dates back to 1287, when the powerful English King Edward I built it as part of his 'iron ring' to repress the rebellious troops of Llewelyn the Great, who had given him a great deal of trouble in his conquest of Wales.

Heading Rooftop Views

Great town walls with gates and towers still encircle old Conwy. You should walk these walls, for they offer a fine rooftop view of the castle, the Conwy Estuary and the rocky knolls of Deganwy, before you arrive at the quayside where you can watch the fishermen sorting their nets and the seagulls watching out for any scraps. The walk description begins at the quayside, not the car park, as you will probably want to take a good look around this medieval town. The route starts on a shoreline path under the boughs of Bodlondeb Wood.

The Ancient Settlements of Conwy Mountain

Not long after passing through Conwy's suburbs you're walking the hillside, on a path threading through gorse and small wind-twisted hawthorns. If you liked the views from the castle walls, you'll love the view from the Conwy Mountain ridge. Looking back you can see the castle, towering over the town's roof tops; but now added to the scene are the Carneddau, the limestone isthmus of the Great Orme and, across the great sands of Lafan, Anglesey.

There is quite a network of paths criss-crossing the ridge and usually the best course is the highest: you'll need to be on the crest path to see the remains of Castell Caer. This 10-acre (4ha) fort has been linked to both Roman and Iron-Age settlers – it certainly has formidable defences, with clearly visible artificial ramparts that overlook spectacular sea cliffs on one side, and a wide view of the land to the south. Beyond the fort, the path misses out the peaks of Penmaen-bach and Alltwen, which is just as well, for the former has been heavily quarried for its roadstone – you probably drove over some of it on your way up the motorway. Instead you should descend to the Sychnant Pass, a splendid, twisting gorge that separates Conwy Mountain from the higher Carneddau peaks.

It's all downhill from here, but the scenery becomes more varied and still maintains interest. As you descend you can see the tidal River Conwy, twisting amongst chequered green fields. Little hills present themselves to you, on your way back north. One last one has pleasant woods with primroses and bluebells, and it gives you another fine view of Conwy Castle to add to your collection before returning to base.

RIGHT: The heather on Mynydd y Dref (Conwy Mountain) slopes gently towards Penmaenbach

walk directions

1 From Conwy Quay head north-west along the waterfront, past the Smallest House and under the town walls. Fork right along a tarmac waterside footpath that rounds Bodlondeb Wood. Turn left along the road, past the school and on to the A547. Cross the road, then the railway line by a footbridge. The track beyond skirts a wood to reach a lane, where you turn right.

2 At a fork bear right past a house to a waymarked stile, from which a footpath rakes up wooded hillsides up on to Conwy Mountain. Follow the undulating crest of Conwy Mountain and continue past Castell Caer.

3 Several tracks converge in the high fields of Pen-Pyra. Here, follow signposts for the North Wales Path along the track heading to the south-west over the left shoulder of Alltwen and down to the metalled road traversing the Sychnant Pass.

4 Follow the footpath from the other side of the road, skirting the woods on your left. Over a stile carry on past Gwern Engen to meet a track. Go right and then bear left, dropping above the Lodge to reach a lane. Turn right along the lane, then turn left, when you reach the next junction, into Groesffordd village. Cross the road, then take the road ahead that swings to the right past a telephone box, then left (south east) towards Plas Iolyn.

5 Turn left at the end but then leave opposite a white house on a path climbing to a cottage. Cross a track and continue upfield to the B5106.

walk information

➤ **DISTANCE**	6.75 miles (10.9km)
➤ **MINIMUM TIME**	4hrs
➤ **ASCENT/GRADIENT**	1,493ft (455m) ▲▲▲
➤ **LEVEL OF DIFFICULTY**	🚶🚶🚶
➤ **PATHS**	Good paths and easy-to-follow moorland tracks, 5 stiles
➤ **LANDSCAPE**	Town, coastline high ridge, farmland and copsee
➤ **SUGGESTED MAPS**	OS Explorer OL17 Snowdon
➤ **START/FINISH**	Grid reference: SH 783775
➤ **DOG FRIENDLINESS**	OK on high ridges, but keep on lead elsewhere
➤ **PARKING**	Large car park on Llanrwst Road behind Conwy Castle
➤ **PUBLIC TOILETS**	At car park

LEFT: Conwy Castle's eight towers and high curtain wall dominate the town of Conwy

Go left to Conwy Touring Park. Follow the drive to a hairpin, from which a waymarked path climbs through trees, recrossing the drive. Finally emerging through a kissing gate, continue up the field edge. Swing left along an undulating ridge above successive pastures, finally meeting a lane.

6 Turn left, shortly leaving right along a track past a communications mast to Bryn-locyn. Continue at the edge of fields beyond to a stile by Coed Benarth, from which a path drops beside the wood.

7 Go over a ladder stile on your left-hand side and descend a field to a roadside gate at the bottom. Turn right on to the B5106 to return to the quayside, or turn left to get back to the main car park.

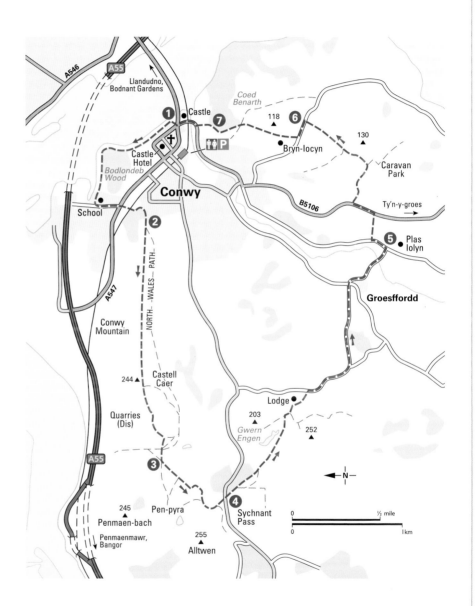

33

A route that takes its time on one of Snowdon's seldom-trod ridges.

Snowdon the Long Way

Llanberis is a slate town, you can see that by looking across Llyn Padarn to the dismal purple-grey terraces built into the mountainside. However it's easy to look the other way, to where Snowdon reigns supreme in the skies.

In Victorian times the interest in mountains was in its infancy. Being Wales' highest peak, attention was centred on Snowdon and the village at its foot.

ABOVE: The round tower at Dolbadarn Castle in Llanberis is built from slate and rubble
LEFT: The Snowdon Mountain Railway with Llanberis in the background

By Train or on Foot

The Snowdon Mountain Railway was built, and opened in 1896 with a fanfare of publicity. Unfortunately, on the first day, a descending train ran out of control and was derailed round a bend, before tumbling down steep slopes. One passenger who jumped from a falling carriage was killed. Since then the steam engines on the rack-and-pinion railway have chugged up the mountain pushing their red and cream carriages for 4.5 miles (7.2km) to the summit without incident. Though a few resent the trains' presence, most walkers are comforted by the whistles that pierce the mountain mists or the plumes of smoke billowing into a blue sky.

The route through the Arddu Valley is a pleasing and peaceful way into the hills. In the early stages you'll ease by the shaly flanks of Moel Eilio before climbing to a dark pass on the Eilio–Snowdon ridge. The mile-long (1.6km) route from the pass to Moel Cynghorion is a bit of a grind, but the summit reveals your prize – a headlong view of Clogwyn Du'r Arddu's black cliffs and several remote tarns basking in two cwms below.

The route joins the Snowdon Ranger Path and zig-zags up Cloggy's rocky arm to Bwlch Glas, where you meet the crowds. Here, you gaze into Cwm Dyli, where the blue-green lakes of Glaslyn and Llydaw lie beneath the ridges of Garnedd Ugain, Crib Goch, and Y Lliwedd.

Now those crowds will lead you alongside the railway to gain the pile of rocks capping Snowdon's highest summit, Yr Wyddfa, where the ugly old summit buildings have been replaced with a new visitor centre. Snowdon's summit panorama is stunning with several peaks in view: you can see half of Wales laid out at your feet. Look further to the distant misty mountains in Ireland and the Isle of Man stretching across the horizon. Our way down Snowdon is easier than the way up: you could even catch the train if you had a mind to. The Llanberis Path is long but it descends in gentle gradients across bare hillsides above the rugged fields of the Arddu Valley.

RIGHT: A view towards Llanberis and Llyn Padarn lake from Glyder Fawr in the Glyderau range

walk directions

1 From the tourist information centre in the heart of Llanberis, head south along the High Street (Stryd Fawr) before turning right up Capel Coch Road. Go straight ahead at a junction, where the road changes its name to Stryd Ceunant, and follow the road past the youth hostel. The road winds and climbs towards Braich y Foel, the north-east spur of Moel Eilio.

2 Where the tarmac ends at the foot of Moel Eilio, continue along the track, which swings left (south-east) into the wild cwm of the Afon Arddu. On the other side of the cwm you'll see the trains of the Snowdon Mountain Railway, puffing up and down the line.

3 On reaching the base of Foel Goch's northern spur, Cefn Drum, the track swings right into Maesgwm and climbs to a pass, Bwlch Maesgwm, between Foel Goch and Moel Cynghorion. Go through the gate here, then turn left and follow the route for the steep climb by the fence and up the latter-mentioned peak.

4 From Cynghorion's summit the route descends along the top of the cliffs of Clogwyn Llechwedd Llo to another pass, Bwlch Cwm Brwynog, which overlooks the small reservoir of Llyn Ffynnon-y-gwas. Here you join the Snowdon Ranger Path.

5 Follow the zig-zag route up Clogwyn Du'r Arddu, whose cliffs, on the left, plummet to a little tarn, Llyn Du'r Arddu, which sits uneasily in a dark stony cwm. Near the top the wide path veers right, away from the edge, meets the Snowdon Mountain Railway, and follows the line to the monolith at Bwlch Glas. Here you are met by both the Llanberis Path and the Pyg Track and look down on the huge cwms of Glaslyn and Llyn Llydaw.

6 The path now follows the line of the railway to the summit. Retrace your steps to Bwlch Glas, but this time follow the wide Llanberis Path traversing the western slopes of Garnedd Ugain and above the railway. (Make sure you don't mistake this for the higher ridge path to Garnedd Ugain's summit.)

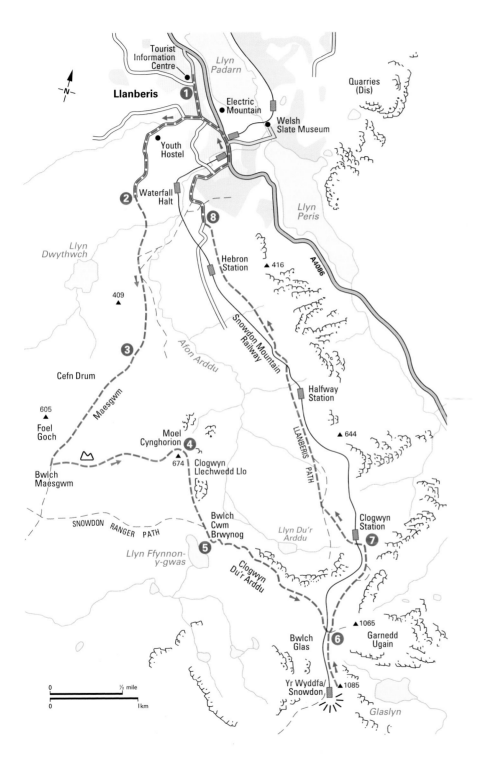

7 Near Clogwyn Station you come to Cwm Hetiau, where cliffs fall away into the chasm of the Pass of Llanberis. The path goes under the railway and below Clogwyn Station before recrossing the line near Halfway Station.

8 The path meets a lane beyond Hebron, and this descends back into Llanberis near the Royal Victoria Hotel. Turn left along the main road, then take the left fork, High Street, to get back to the car.

walk information	
► **DISTANCE**	10 miles (16.1km)
► **MINIMUM TIME**	6hrs 30min
► **ASCENT/GRADIENT**	3,839ft (1,170m) ▲▲▲
► **LEVEL OF DIFFICULTY**	🌂🌂🌂
► **PATHS**	Well-defined paths and tracks, 1 stile
► **LANDSCAPE**	High mountain cwms and tarnss
► **SUGGESTED MAPS**	OS Explorer OL17 Snowdon
► **START/FINISH**	Grid reference: SH 577604
► **DOG FRIENDLINESS**	Sheep, trains and crags: best on lead throughout
► **PARKING**	Several car parks throughout Llanberis
► **PUBLIC TOILETS**	Just off High Street, south of tourist information centre

LEFT: The chasm in the Llanberis pass

Explore the most perfect hanging valley in Snowdonia, its rock ledges and hanging gardens.

A Taming Walk in the Devil's Kitchen

ABOVE: Hikers make their way along the Carneddau range
LEFT: Mount Tryfan from Ogwen Valley

Shepherds say that Idwal is the haunt of demons and no bird dares fly over its damned water. In the 18th century, writer Thomas Pennant came here and said it was 'a place to inspire murderous thoughts, environed with horrible precipices', and it was here in the 12th century that Idwal, son of Owain Gwynedd, was brutally murdered by Dunawd, in whose care he had been entrusted.

Menacing Atmosphere

If you come to this place on a day when the damp mountain mists swirl in and out of the blackened mossy crags, and when rain-soaked waterfalls drop from those mists like plumes of steam, you will experience the atmospheric menace. However, the sunshine can paint a very different picture, with golden rocks that are a playground for the modern-day climber and small mountain birds such as the wheatear and ring ouzel flitting through the breeze-blown grasses.

A Perfect Hanging Valley

Cwm Idwal is a perfect hanging valley, and a fine place to study geology and nature. In the last ice age a small glacier would have been slowly scouring its way over the cliffs at the head of the cwm before joining the huge glacier that used to fill the U-shaped valley of Nant Ffrancon. You will pass the moraines (the debris left behind by the glacier) not long after leaving the car park at Ogwen.

The glaciation left a legacy in Idwal, for here in the inaccessible places free from animal grazing, rare plant species are to be found. These brought botanists from far and wide. Their favoured spots were the crags around Twll Du, otherwise known as the Devil's Kitchen, a deep defile where the mountainside's volcanic bedrock is divided by a column of basalt. Here was the snout of the glacier and, on the surrounding ledges and crevices, the rich soils allowed many species of Arctic plants to flourish. The most famous is the rare Snowdon lily, discovered in the 17th century by Edward Llwyd. Tufted and Arctic saxifrage are also here, but hard to spot, but the starry and mossy saxifrages are there for all to see, as are wood sorrel, wood anemone and oak ferns. Collectively, the foliage seems to flow down the rocks and you can see why it's called the Hanging Gardens.

Lofty Viewpoint

Climbing above the rocks the path attains a wild and windswept hollow of moor grass and rushes. Llyn y Cwn (dog lake) is a shallow pool tucked beneath the loose boulder and shale slopes of Glyder Fawr.

In summer bogbean rings the pool's outer edges with its pale pink blooms. This is a fine lofty place to dwell and admire the mountain views before going back down to the cauldron of Idwal.

walk directions

1 The Cwm Idwal nature trail starts to the left of the toilet block at Ogwen and climbs up the hillside to pass some impressive waterfalls before turning right and continuing up the hill.

2 Go through a gate in a fence, that marks the boundary of the National Nature Reserve, and turn left along the side of Llyn Idwal's eastern shores. The clear footpath climbs into the dark shadows of Cwm Idwal.

3 Now you leave the nature trail, which turns right to complete a circuit around the lake. Instead ascend beneath the rock climbing grounds of the Idwal Slabs and across the stream of Nant Ifan, beyond which the footpath zig-zags up rough boulder ground to the foot of Twll Du – the Devil's Kitchen. If the weather, and the forecast too, are fine climb to Llyn y Cwn at the top of this impressive defile, if not, skip this bit and go to Point 6.

4 To ascend Twll Du climb the engineered path as it angles left up the rock face, which will now be on your right-hand side, above an extensive area of scree and boulder. At the top you come to a relatively gentle (by comparison) grassy hollow between the rising summits of Y Garn, to the right, and Glyder Fawr, to the left.

5 Just beyond the first grassy mounds you come across the small tarn of Llyn y Cwn – the dog lake – which makes a great picnic spot. Now retrace your steps carefully to the bottom of Twll Du.

6 Among some huge boulders, the path forks and the left branch heads down to run above the western shore of Llyn Idwal, then rounds its northern end to meet the outward route at Point 2. Now follow the route of your outward journey back to the car park at Ogwen.

walk information

➤ **DISTANCE**	3 miles (4.8km)
➤ **MINIMUM TIME**	2hrs 30min
➤ **ASCENT/GRADIENT**	1,378ft (420m) ▲▲▲
➤ **LEVEL OF DIFFICULTY**	林林林
➤ **PATHS**	Well-defined paths
➤ **LANDSCAPE**	High mountain cwm
➤ **SUGGESTED MAPS**	OS Explorer OL17 Snowdon
➤ **START/FINISH**	Grid reference: SH 649603
➤ **DOG FRIENDLINESS**	Dogs should be on lead
➤ **PARKING**	Small pay car park at Ogwen; others along Llyn Ogwene
➤ **PUBLIC TOILETS**	At car park

ABOVE: There are numerous campsites around Snowdonia, such as this one below the summit of Tryfan in the Ogwen Valley

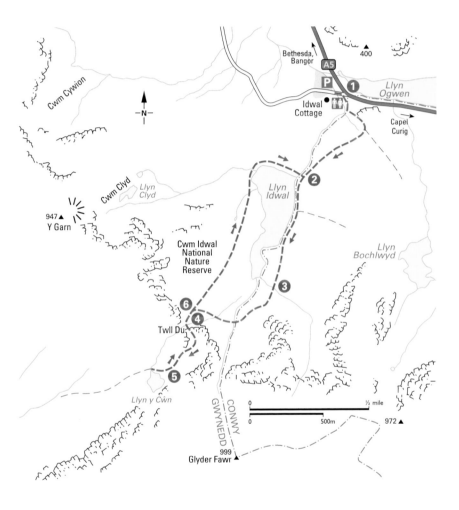

*Discovering the valley where
rocks and the mountains are
still all important.*

An Alpine Journey Above the Llugwy

ABOVE: *A ruined farmhouse near Capel Curig*
LEFT: *The reflective waters of Llynau Mymbyr
lake near Capel Curig*

*'I descended a great steep into Glan Llugwy, a bottom watered
by the Llugwy, fertile in grass and varied by small groves of
young oaks… The small church of Capel Curig, and a few
scattered houses give life to this dreary tract. Yr Wyddfa and
all his sons, Crib Goch, Crib y Ddysgl, Lliwedd, Yr Aran and
many others here burst at once into full view and make this
the finest approach to our boasted Alps'*
Thomas Pennant, A Tour in Wales, 1778

The description holds true today, for
nowhere has one village been so strung
out – Capel Curig's sparse cottages and
inns stretch 6 miles (9.7km) between Pont-
Cyfyng, beneath Moel Siabod, to the Pen y
Gwryd, beneath Glyder Fawr.

A New Breed of Visitor

The link still lies in those alps. The well-spaced inns were positioned there, at first to serve the quarrymen from the barracks of Siabod and the miners from the copper mines of Snowdon, then, when the mines and quarries shut down, that new breed of visitor, the walker and the climber. These inns were a convenient meeting place. Geoffrey Winthrop Young was one of the first, but many followed, pioneering new routes on the crags. Quickly Capel Curig became the Zermatt of Wales, and Snowdon, the Matterhorn. In the 1950s the Pen y Gwryd Inn, run by enthusiast Chris Biggs, became a centre for planning Alpine and Himalayan expeditions. Here Lord Hunt and his team, who in 1953 were the first to climb Everest, met to make the final preparations before departing for Nepal. The Climbers' Bar has a wood ceiling that has been autographed by many world famous climbers, including the summit pair, Sir Edmund Hillary and Tenzing Norgay.

This walk will round the valley, taking in views of the wide sweep of mountains that surround Capel Curig and the Llugwy Valley.

To the Woods

You continue through those oak woods seen by Pennant, now wonderfully matured, before descending back down to the boisterous river. In front of the Ty'n y Coed Inn they have one of the old London to Holyhead stagecoaches on display. After crossing the river at Pont-Cyfyng you follow its delightful banks for a short while, then go over crag, across pasture and through the woods. You come out by a footbridge on the shores of Llynnau Mymbyr, and again you see Snowdon, maybe still perfectly reflected in glass-like waters. On the other side of the bridge at the Plas y Brenin National Mountain Centre, they're training the next generation of mountaineers.

RIGHT: Capel Curig from across the blue waters of Llyn y Mymbyr lake

walk directions

1 The path begins at a ladder stile by the war memorial on the A5 and climbs towards Y Pincin, a large craggy outcrop cloaked in wood and bracken. Go over another stile and keep to the left of the outcrop.

Those who want to go to the top should do so from the north-east, where the gradients are easier. It's fun, but take care! You'll need to retrace your steps to the main route.

LEFT: Capel Curig (foreground) is located in the heart of Snowdonia; Mount Snowdon looms in the distance

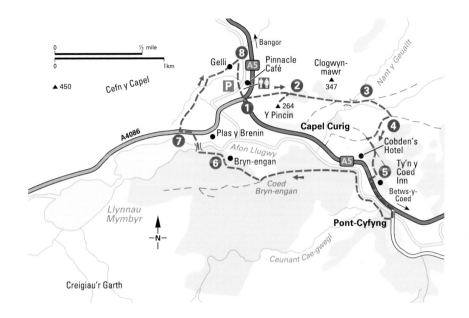

2 Continue east through woods and across marshy ground, keeping well to the right of the great crags of Clogwyn-mawr. On reaching a couple of ladder stiles, ignore the footpath, right, back down to the road, but maintain your direction across the hillside.

3 Just beyond a footbridge over Nant y Geuallt, leave the main footpath and follow a less well-defined one, with marker posts, across marshy ground. This path veers south-east to cross another stream before coming to a prominent track.

4 Turn right along the track, go over a ladder stile, then at a four-way meeting of paths head left. Follow the path descending into some woods. Take the right-hand fork descending to the road near Ty'n y Coed Inn.

5 Turn left down the road, then right, along the lane over Pont-Cyfyng. Go right again beyond the bridge to follow a footpath that traces the Llugwy to another bridge opposite Cobdens Hotel. Don't cross this time, but scramble left over some rocks before continuing through the woods of Coed Bryn-engan, where the path soon becomes a wide track.

6 After passing the cottage of Bryn-engan, the track comes to the bridge at the head of the Mymbyr lakes. Turn right across it, then go left along the road for a short way.

7 Cross the road to the next ladder stile and take a track straight ahead, soon swinging right to hug the foot of the southern Glyder slopes.

8 When you get beyond Gelli farm turn right to follow the cart track back to the car park.

walk information

➤ **DISTANCE**	4 miles (6.4km)
➤ **MINIMUM TIME**	2hrs
➤ **ASCENT/GRADIENT**	295ft (90m)
➤ **LEVEL OF DIFFICULTY**	(doesn't include pinnacle scramble)
➤ **PATHS**	Generally clear and surfaced but can be wet in places, 9 stiles
➤ **LANDSCAPE**	Woodland, wetland and high pasture
➤ **SUGGESTED MAPS**	OS Explorer OL17 Snowdon
➤ **START/FINISH**	Grid reference: SJ 720582
➤ **DOG FRIENDLINESS**	Dogs should be on lead
➤ **PARKING**	Behind Joe Brown's shop at Capel Curig
➤ **PUBLIC TOILETS**	By Joe Brown's shop

A walk up to the old copper mines of Mynydd Sygyn and through the spectacular Pass of Aberglaslyn.

There's Copper in Them There Hills

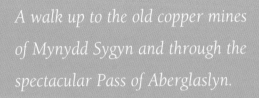

This route heads for the rugged hills forming one side of the great Aberglaslyn gorge that has graced many a postcard and book jacket. At the back of the car park you pass under a railway bridge that belonged to the Welsh Highland Railway and pass the site of an old crushing plant. Here, copper ore from the mountain would have been prepared for shipment, using the railway.

ABOVE: The fast flowing Afon Glaslyn, cuts its way towards the flat fields of Traeth Mawr
LEFT: The Afon Glaslyn river towards Aberglaslyn Gorge

51

Cwm Bychan

Beyond the plant, the path follows a playful stream and climbs steadily through the lonely Cwm Bychan. Here, beneath splintered, craggy mountains patched with heather and bracken, you come across a line of rusting gantries. They're part of an old aerial ropeway, built to carry ore down to the crushing mill. Mining had taken place hereabouts since Roman times, but after World War One the extraction became uneconomical. In 1922 the mines closed.

Continuing to the col above, the route comes to a huge area of mining spoil and a meeting of routes. Ours turns south, and soon we're following a rugged rocky path zig-zagging down to a grassy basin below before continuing along a craggy ridge. Here the ground drops away steeply into the valley of the Afon Glaslyn. If it's early summer the scene will be emblazoned by the vivid pink blooms of rhododendrons, which smother the hillside. Hundreds of feet below lie the roof tops of Beddgelert and what lies in-between is a glorious little path twisting through those rhododendrons and the rocks into the village. If you get that feeling of déjà vu the hillsides around here were used for the setting of the Chinese village in The Inn of the Sixth Happiness (1958), starring Ingrid Bergman.

Beddgelert is a pretty village with a fine two-arched bridge spanning the Glaslyn and a handful of busy craft shops and cafés, which throng with visitors in the summer. Around here they're all too fond of telling you the story of Prince Llewelyn's brave dog, Gelert, and pointing to the grave which gave the village its name. Don't be misled; a past landlord of the Royal Goat devised the plausible story to boost his trade. We're going to head for the great gorge of Aberglaslyn!

The Gorge

The way back to Aberglaslyn used to be by way of the old Welsh Highland Railway trackbed, but since this has been reopened the only route is now a rough track by the raging river. The hard bit with handholds comes early on. If you can manage that you can enjoy the excitement of a walk through the gorge and through the attractive woodland that shades its banks. If you want to see that postcard view though, you'll have to make a short detour to the roadside at Pont Aberglaslyn. It's stunning if you haven't seen it before.

walk information

➤ DISTANCE	4 miles (6.4km)
➤ MINIMUM TIME	2hrs 30min
➤ ASCENT/GRADIENT	1,181ft (360m) ▲▲▲
➤ LEVEL OF DIFFICULTY	✹✹✹✹
➤ PATHS	Well-maintained paths and tracks (see note below), 2 stiles
➤ LANDSCAPE	Rocky hills and river gorge
➤ SUGGESTED MAPS	OS Explorer OL17 Snowdon
➤ START/FINISH	Grid reference: SH 597462
➤ DOG FRIENDLINESS	Dogs should be on lead at all times
➤ PARKING	National Trust pay car park, Aberglaslyn
➤ PUBLIC TOILETS	At car park
➤ NOTE	Short section of riverside path in Aberglaslyn gorge is difficult and requires use of handholds

walk directions

1 The path starts to the left of the toilet block and goes under the old railway bridge, before climbing through Cwm Bychan. After a steady climb the path reaches the iron pylons of the aerial cableway.

2 Beyond the pylons, keep straight on, ignoring paths forking left. A grassy corridor leads to a col, where there's a stile in a fence that is not shown on current maps. Bear left beyond the stile and head for a three-way footpath signpost by the rocks of Grib Ddu.

3 Follow the path on the left signed 'To Beddgelert and Sygun' and go over another ladder stile. Turn left, then follow the path down round a rocky knoll and then down the hillside to a signpost. Just beyond the sign is the cairn at Bwlch-y-Sygyn and over to the left is a shallow, peaty pool in a green hollow.

4 The path now heads south-west along the mountain's north-western ridge, overlooking Beddgelert. Ignore any lesser paths along the way.

5 Watch out for a large cairn, highlighting the turn-off right for Beddgelert. The clear stony path weaves through rhododendron and rock, goes through a kissing gate in a wall half-way down, then descends further to the edge of Beddgelert, where a little lane passing the cottage of Penlan leads to the Afon Glaslyn.

6 Turn left to follow the river for a short way. Don't cross the footbridge over the river but turn left to follow the Glaslyn's east bank. Cross the restored railway line and then continue between it and the river.

7 Below the first tunnel, the path is pushed right to the water's edge. Handholds screwed into the rocks assist passage on a difficult but short section. The path continues through riverside woodland and over boulders until it comes to Pont Aberglaslyn.

8 Here, turn left up some steps and follow a dirt path through the woods. Just before the railway, follow a signed path down and right to the car park.

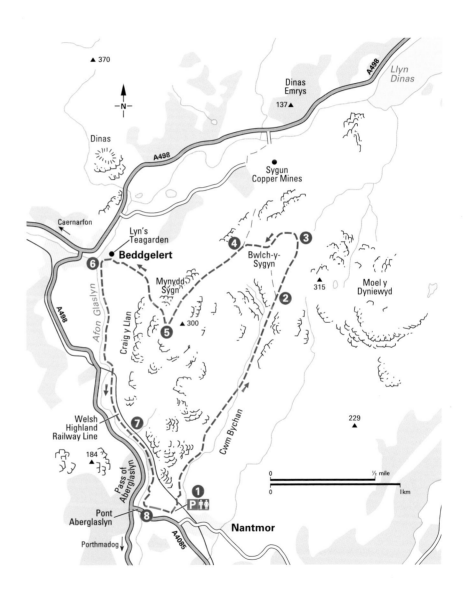

Cwm Bychan is one of the treasures
of Snowdonia and the Roman Steps
one of its oldest highways.

With the Drovers Over the Roman Steps

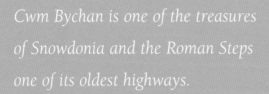

The road from Llanbedr into Cwm Bychan is a joy in itself, passing through oak woods, by the banks of a babbling stream and beneath the small rocky castles of the Rhinog foothills. Llyn Cwm Bychan is stunning. If you see it on an August day, when the colourful heather contrasts with the vivid green of the sessile oaks, and the clouds' shadows play on the rocks of Carreg-y-saeth, then you've seen most of what is good about the Rhinogs.

ABOVE: The Roman Steps work their way down
towards Cwm Bychan in the Rhinogs
LEFT: Traditionally known as the Roman Steps
due to their supposed use by Roman Sentries,
the steps actually date back to medieval times

Up Those Steps

It seems a shame to lose the paradise that is Cwm Bychan, but we lose it for the shade of its oak woods. As the path climbs towards the Rhinog crags its surface becomes one of great rock slabs that form steps. These Roman Steps are in fact part of a medieval packhorse track, though the Romans, who had a fort in the Trawsfynydd area, might well have used their predecessors. Drovers would have passed this way too, on their way from Harlech to the markets in England, picking up local herds of Welsh Black cattle on the way.

The climb into the pass of Bwlch Tyddiad takes you into country that resembles the canyons of Utah or Arizona. Bwlch Tyddiad narrows and the walls of the surrounding hills close in. Suddenly you're at the top of the pass and looking across a huge rushy hollow surrounded by a million spruce trees, part of the Coed-y-Brenin forest. The trees provide cover for the next couple of miles as the route heads northwards along the east side of the ridge.

From Moel y Gwartheg at the northern edge of the forest there's a good view of the knobbly northern Rhinog ridge and the huge Trawsfynydd reservoir. The Magnox nuclear power station on the far side is being decommissioned now, but the lake used to emit steam into the air as it was used by the station for cooling purposes. Controversy still rages, for they're considering turning the site into a nuclear waste plant. A slow and painstaking operation will restore the site to a greenfield status. It is hoped to be completed by 2098!

Paradise Regained

The last stretch of the walk climbs back over another wild heathery pass tucked beneath the craggy mountains of Clip and Craig Wion. From here the path, a narrow ribbon of peat, winds its way through the heather to make a return to the greenery of Cwm Bychan, where paradise is regained.

walk directions

1 Go through the gate at the back of the car park at Llyn Cwm Bychan and over the paved causeway across the stream. Beyond a stile the path climbs up through an area of squat woodland.

2 Over another stile you leave woodland behind and cross a stream on a small bridge. The path, always clear, climbs steadily to a gate. Now slabbed with 'the steps', it climbs through a heather-clad rocky ravine and on to the cairn marking the highest point along the rocky pass of Bwlch Tyddiad.

3 From the col, the path descends into a grassy moorland basin beneath Rhinog Fawr, then, beyond a stile, enters the conifers of the Coed-y-Brenin plantation. A well-defined footpath tucks away under the trees and eventually comes to a wide flinted forestry road, along which you turn left.

4 After about a mile (1.6 km), the road swings away to head east; watch out for a way-marked path on the left just beyond the turn. Waymarks guide the route left, then right, to pass the ruins of Hafod-Gynfal. Beyond this you head north to go over a ladder stile and out of the forest.

5 Go straight ahead from the stile, heading north across the grassy moor of Moel y Gwartheg. The ground gets wet as you descend, but it's wetter still further right. You're heading for the isolated cottage of Wern-fach, which stands a little to the left of a small patch of conifers, but for now aim towards the green fields of Cefn Clawdd.

6 You meet a fence, which guides you down to Wern-fâch. Cross a stile, then just above the cottage turn left and go over two ladder stiles. Follow the main stream (Afon Crawcwellt) to Wern-cyfrdwy (house), pass behind it,

then join the walls and fences that shadow the stream. These give the least wet line across the sodden moorland.

7 The going firms up as the ground steepens, climbing to the lonely col of Bwlch Gwylim, a narrow pass between Clip and Craig Wion. Descending the far side, Cwm Bychan and the start of the walk come back into view. The footpath now descends to the south-west, through heather and bracken. After a ladder stile, look for a small waymark where you turn left down steep slopes back to the car park.

walk information

➤ **DISTANCE**	7 miles (11.3km)
➤ **MINIMUM TIME**	5hrs
➤ **ASCENT/GRADIENT**	1,575ft (480m)
➤ **LEVEL OF DIFFICULTY**	
➤ **PATHS**	Rocky paths, tracks and boggy moorland, 9 stiles
➤ **LANDSCAPE**	Gnarled gritstone peaks with heather slopes
➤ **SUGGESTED MAPS**	OS Explorer OL18 Harlech, Porthmadog & Bala
➤ **START/FINISH**	Grid reference: SH 646314
➤ **DOG FRIENDLINESS**	Can be off lead in upper heather-clad regions of walk
➤ **PARKING**	Llyn Cwm Bychan
➤ **PUBLIC TOILETS**	Portaloo at car park
➤ **NOTE**	The moorlands around the eastern end of the walk can be very wet and dangerous, with streams under the bogland. The walk is best tackled after a long dry spell

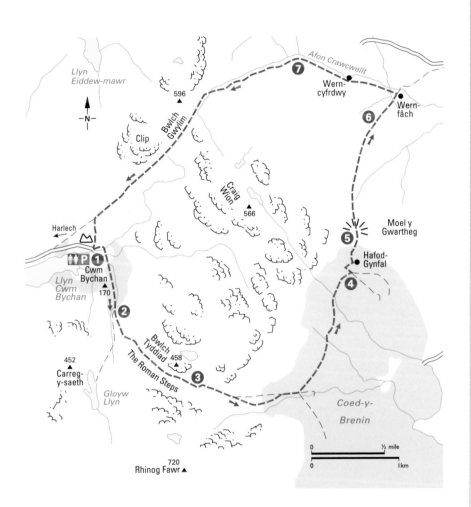

*One of the finest short walks in Wales, the
Precipice Walk follows a balcony route with
spectacular views of valley, mountain and estuary.*

A Stroll Around the Precipice

*ABOVE: Precipice Walk at Dolgellau
LEFT: The Dolgellau countryside is famous
for its unspoilt beauty*

There's been a house at Nannau since the 12th century, when the estate was owned by descendants of Cadwgan, Prince of Powys. That original building was burned down in 1404 after trouble between the owner, Hywel Sele, the 8th Lord of Nannau and his cousin Owain Glyndwr. The pair had never liked or trusted each other, mainly due to Hywel's allegiance to England's House of Lancaster, but they were brought together by the Abbot of Cymer (the abbey in the valley below).

Owain and Hywel

While out hunting together Glyndwr spotted a doe and pointed it out for Hywel, who was a fine bowman, to kill. Hywel pretended to aim at the animal but then suddenly swung around towards Owain. The arrow was straight and true but, as Glyndwr had been wearing armour under his tunic, it did not pierce his skin. After burning down the house it is said that Glyndwr killed his cousin and disposed of his body in a hollow tree. The skeleton wasn't found for 40 years and the house wasn't rebuilt until 1693.

The Nannau family, who became the Nanneys, still lived on the estate, but had financial problems. Hugh Nanney was heavily fined and imprisoned for trying to resolve his difficulties by felling 10,000 oaks. When the male line died out the female line, which had married into the powerful Vaughan family, took over. The Vaughans replanted many of the trees and, in 1796, built the grand mansion that you see today.

Spectacular Views

As you start high there's very little ascent to do and the early part of the walk eases across woodland and farm pastures. As the path rounds Foel Cynwch and past the Sitka spruce of Coed Dôl-y-clochydd, spectacular views of the wooded Mawddach and Wen valleys open up. The high ridge seen on the other side of the Mawddach is Y Garn, one of the Rhinog outliers. It looks a gentle enough walk from here, but Y Garn's other face is of thick heather and precipitous rock.

Exciting Terrace

Beyond another ladder stile the path itself gets spectacular, taking the form of an exciting terrace, high above the river. Crag, the odd birch and rowan, and flecks of pink from rhododendron bushes all decorate a magnificent scene, which soon adds the great northern cliffs of the Cadair Idris mountains to its repertoire. The precipice lasts an exquisite mile (1.6km) with little twists and turns to add a little spice to the walk. Before long you can trace the Mawddach past Dolgellau's plains, past the sandbars of its estuary, to the sea beyond.

Old Oak Trees

It seems a shame to leave all this behind, but the little path veers left and descends to the shores of Llyn Cynwch where anglers will be casting for trout. The lake also has an avenue of old oak trees, all that remains of what was quite a large forest until Hugh Nanney took to his axe. When you reach the far shores of the lake stop to take one last look south. Here you will see the cliffs of Cadair Idris reflected and rippling with the lapping waters of the lake.

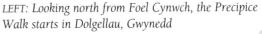
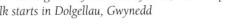

LEFT: Looking north from Foel Cynwch, the Precipice Walk starts in Dolgellau, Gwynedd

LEFT: The view south along Llyn Cynwch river

walk directions

1 From the top end of the car park turn right on a level footpath which curves around to join another wide track. The Precipice Walk is a private path around the Nannau Estate, but its use has been authorised by the estate owners since 1890, on the basis that all walkers observe the country code. It's probably one of the finest short routes in Wales and, as such, has been one of Dolgellau's most famous attractions since those early days when Victorian tourists came for their constitutional perambulations. The track swings right at the edge of some fields.

2 Where the track comes to an estate cottage, Gwern-offeiriaid, turn left off it. Follow a clear path leading to the hillside north of Llyn Cynwch. There you see the grand mansion of Nannau, built for the Vaughans in 1796.

3 At a footpath signpost fork right. The path climbs the hillside and turns northwards by the side of a dry-stone wall.

4 Beyond a stile the footpath curves around a crag-studded hill, with open slopes that give fine views across a green valley below to the village of Llanfachreth and the rugged mountainsides of Rhobell Fawr and Dduallt that lie behind. The footpath edges rounds Foel Cynwch and passes the Sitka spruce woodlands of Coed Dôl-y-clochydd. Ignore a path signed to Glasdir and keep left, reaching the dramatic, but even ledge path traversing the high hill slopes above the Mawddach Valley. Where the slopes finally ease, there's

walk information

➤ **DISTANCE**	3 miles (4.8km)
➤ **MINIMUM TIME**	2hrs
➤ **ASCENT/GRADIENT**	Negligible
➤ **LEVEL OF DIFFICULTY**	
➤ **PATHS**	Stony tracks and good paths, occasionally rough, 4 stiles
➤ **LANDSCAPE**	Mountainside and pasture
➤ **SUGGESTED MAPS**	OS Explorer OL18 Harlech, Porthmadog & Bala
➤ **START/FINISH**	Grid reference: SH 745211
➤ **DOG FRIENDLINESS**	Private land – dogs must always be on a lead
➤ **PARKING**	Coed y Groes car park on Dolgellau–Llanfachreth road
➤ **PUBLIC TOILETS**	At car park
➤ **NOTE**	Wear strong footwear as part of route follows narrow path with big drops down to Mawddach Valley. Not a walk for vertigo sufferers

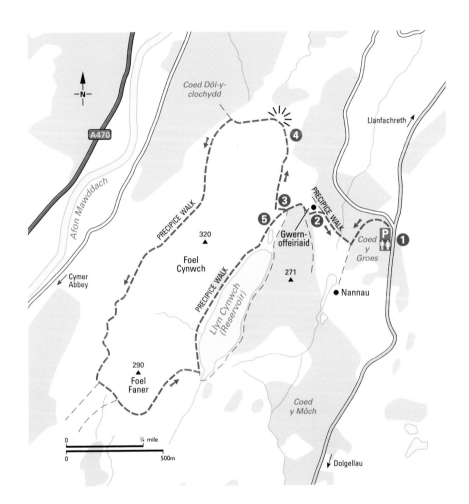

a promontory on the right, with a bench placed to enjoy the view. The path now arcs round to the southern side of Foel Faner, drops to the lake and turns sharp left to follow the western shore.

5 The path meets the outward route by the hill footpath sign. Retrace the outward route past the estate cottage of Gwern-offeiriaid and through the woods back to the car park.

Walk in the footsteps of Wordsworth,
Darwin and Ruskin who visited here
to work and to explore.

The Sublime Mawddach

Barmouth (once better known in Welsh as Y Bermo), used to be a seaport, trading the coarse woollen goods of Merionydd with the Americas. In those days the village cottages were strung out across terraces in the cliffs and there was one pub, the Corsygedol Arms, for the traveller. There wasn't enough room to squeeze the main road from Harlech between those rocks and the sea, so it bypassed the village and instead went inland, over the Rhinog mountain passes.

ABOVE: Pretty cottages add to Barmouth's charm
LEFT: Sandbanks in the Afon Mawddach Estuary
near Penmaenpool reveal themselves at low tide

Barmouth: the New Era

In the mid-19th century it all changed. Barmouth built a main street on the beach. Visitors became more frequent and the resort's sea and sand attracted the gentry from the Midlands. Barmouth also came to the notice of the famous: the poet, Wordsworth said of the Mawddach Estuary that it was sublime and equal to any in Scotland. Artists like J M W Turner and Richard Wilson came to capture the changing light and renowned beauty of estuary and mountainside.

In 1867 the railway came, and a new bridge was engineered across the estuary sands. It was half a mile (800m) long and had a swing section across the Mawddach's main channel to allow shipping to pass. Today you can see that Barmouth is not as smart as it was in its heyday. It's still in the most wonderful situation though and, as you step on to the wooden boards of that half-mile foot and railway bridge, you can feel exactly what Wordsworth felt.

Mighty Cadair Idris

The view is best when the sun's shining and the tide's half out. That way the waters of the Mawddach will be meandering like a pale blue serpent amid pristine golden sandbars. Your eyes cannot help but be drawn to mighty Cadair Idris. This is not one mountain, but a long ridge with several peaks, each displaying fierce cliffs that soar above the wooded foothills. The biggest is Penygadair at 2,927ft (893m), but the most prominent is Tyrrau Mawr, a shapely peak with a seemingly overhanging crag. As you get to the other side you can look back to Barmouth, and you will see how this town has been built into the rocks of the lower Rhinogs. Across the bridge you're ready to explore those wooded foothills. Through Arthog the path climbs between oak trees and you find yourself looking across to some waterfalls, thundering into a wooded chasm. At the top you are presented with an elevated view of all that you have seen so far, the estuary, the sandbars, the mountains and the yawning bridge.

RIGHT: Boats moored in the blue waters of Barmouth
Estuary near the Barmouth Bridge, Gwynedd

walk directions

ABOVE: Afon Mawddach Estuary at low tide; the area was known for ship building in the 18th century

1 Follow the promenade round the harbour, then go over the footbridge across the estuary (toll). On reaching the path along the south shore of the estuary, turn left to follow the grassy embankment that leads to a track rounding the wooded knoll of Fegla Fawr on its seaward side.

2 Reaching the terraced houses of Mawddach Crescent, follow the track that passes to their rear. Rejoin the track along the shoreline until you reach a gate on the right marking the start of a bridleway heading inland across the marshes of Arthog.

3 Turn left along the old railway track, then leave it just before the crossing of the little Arthog Estuary and turn right along a tarmac lane by a small car park. Bear left over a ladder stile and follow a raised embankment to a wall which now leads the path to the main Dolgellau road next to St Catherine's Church.

4 Opposite the church gate is a footpath beginning with some steps into woodland. A good waymarked path now climbs by the Arthog.

walk information

➤ **DISTANCE**	6 miles (9.7km)
➤ **MINIMUM TIME**	4hrs
➤ **ASCENT/GRADIENT**	656ft (200m) ▲▲△
➤ **LEVEL OF DIFFICULTY**	🚶🚶🚶
➤ **PATHS**	A bridge, good tracks and woodland paths, 6 stiles
➤ **LANDSCAPE**	Estuary and wooded hills
➤ **SUGGESTED MAPS**	OS Explorer OL23 Cadair Idris & Llyn Tegid
➤ **START/FINISH**	Grid reference: SH 613155
➤ **DOG FRIENDLINESS**	Dogs should be on lead at all times
➤ **PARKING**	Car park on seafront
➤ **PUBLIC TOILETS**	At Barmouth's car park, or near Morfa Mawddach Station

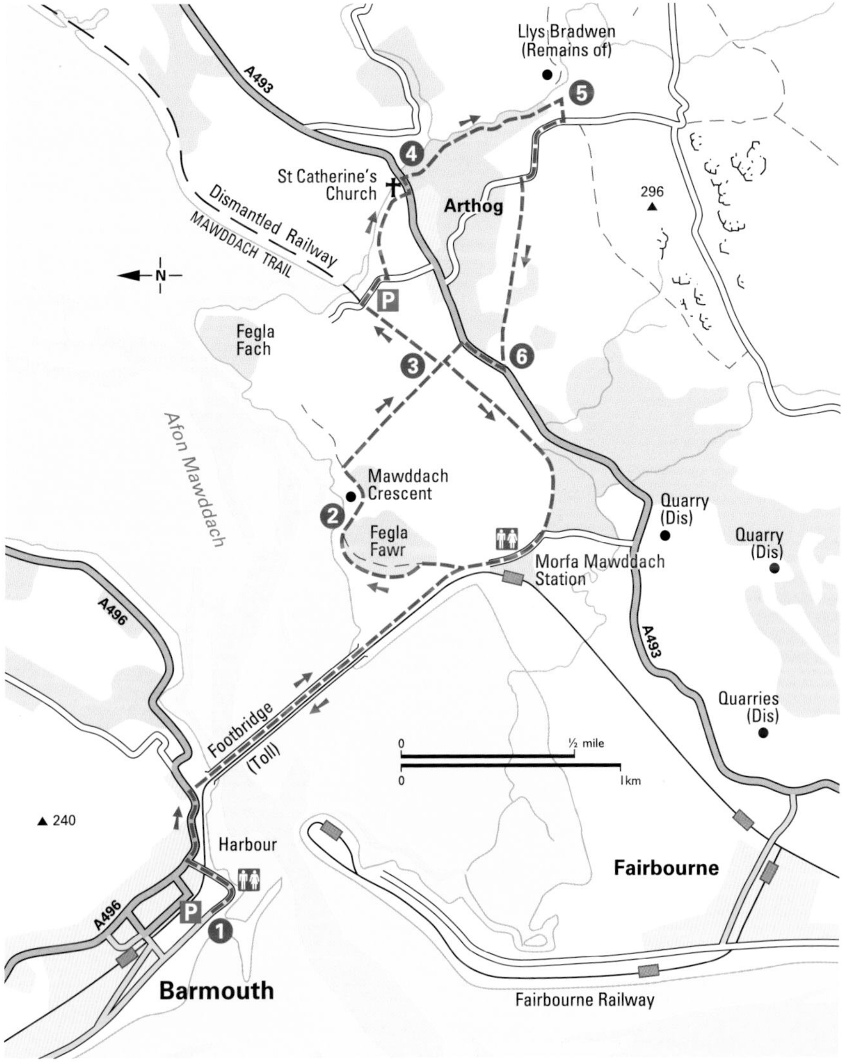

5 Beyond a stile at the top of the woods, turn right to come to a lane. Turn right along the descending lane, then left along a stony track passing the cottage of Merddyn. The track gets narrower and steeper as it descends into more woodland, beneath the boulders of an old quarry and down to the Dolgellau road by Arthog Village Hall.

6 Turn right along the road, then left along a path back to the railway track and the Mawddach Trail. Turn left along the trail and follow it past Morfa Mawddach Station and back across Barmouth's bridge.

Explore the valleys where the princes of Wales held out against Edward I and a barefoot girl inspired a world-renowned society.

The Dysynni Valley and Castell y Bere

ABERGYNOLWYN lies in the emerald valley of the Dysynni and beneath the great spruce woods of the Dyfi Forest. It's a village built out of Welsh slate and from the proceeds of that slate. However, on this walk we turn our backs on the purple rock to head northwards for the rolling green hills and the delectable oak woods of Coed Cedris that cloak their lower slopes. At the top of these woods you're transported into a high cwm. The Nant yr Eira trickles out from the rushes, but by the time you're descending into the valley of the Cadair, it's splashing and cascading through its own shady ravine.

ABOVE: *Castell y Bere near Cadair Idris*
LEFT: *The viewpoint below Foel Fawr at Furnace*

Mary Jones

Through more woodland, you come to the valley bottom at Llanfihangel-y-pennant, where there's an attractive stone-built chapel that dates back to the 12th century. These days it's dedicated to Mary Jones, a poor weaver's daughter of the 18th century. As a 15-year-old she decided she wanted a Welsh-language Bible of her own. Though she had no shoes to wear, Mary made her way across hills to Bala, some 30 miles (48km) away, where she had heard that some were available. Unfortunately for Mary, the Revd Thomas Charles had none left to sell but, touched by her persistence, he gave her his own copy. Charles was very impressed by Mary's tenacity and it inspired him to consider the needs of Christians around the world who couldn't read the Bible in their own language. Along with several like-minded evangelicals, in 1804 he founded a group called the British and Foreign Bible Society. As well as Bibles in Welsh, one of the first they produced was in Mohawk. Mary's cottage, Tyn-y-ddol, and a monument to her, can be found a short way north up the road.

Welsh Fortress

The main route heads in the opposite direction. Here the Afon Cadair has formed a wide flat valley. In the middle of the plains, perched on a great crag are the ruins of a true Welsh fortress, Castell y Bere. Built in the early 13th century by Llewelyn the Great, it held out longer than any other when Edward I and his armies invaded Wales. By this time Llewelyn ap Grufydd had become Prince of Wales, but had been killed at Builth, leaving his brother Dafydd to defend the castle. Dafydd fought long and hard but was defeated in 1283.

He escaped capture for a while and hid out on the slopes of Cadair Idris. Eventually, he was betrayed by his own people and was dragged to Shrewsbury where he was brutally hung, drawn and quartered. So Wales was defeated and the castle laid waste.

Narrow Defile

The path continues along the now peaceful pastures of this pleasant valley to meet the Dysynni which has wriggled through a narrow defile between two hills. The winding green track that squeezes through with it is perhaps the finest mile in this book; you're almost disappointed to get back to Abergynolwyn so soon.

walk directions

1 Cross the road to the Railway Inn and take the lane signposted to Llanegryn. At the far side of the bridge spanning the Dysynni river, turn right through a kissing gate and trace above the north banks. At a second step stile the path turns left before climbing some steps alongside some tall leylandii to reach a country lane.

2 Turn right along the lane which heads east through the Dysynni Valley and beneath the woodlands of Coed Meriafel. At the junction with the B4405 turn left, over a stile and climb north-west across a field. Continue over two more stiles to a woodland path. Follow this to reach a forestry track near the top of the woods.

3 Turn left along the track which climbs out of the woods before veering right to a gate and adjacent stile, giving entry into a large field. Go straight ahead to pick up a ruined overgrown wall. Where this ends, bear left to descend a high grassy cwm with a stream developing just to your left. Ford another stream which joins from the right near a ruin.

4 The green path develops a flinted surface. Leave it where it starts to climb and rejoin a streamside path on the left. This descends into the woods and stays close to the stream. After passing several cascades it comes out of the woods to reach a track, which in turn leads to the road at Llanfihangel-y-pennant just opposite the chapel.

5 Turn left past the chapel and Castell y Bere (detour through gates on the right for a closer look). Just beyond the castle, take a path on the left that climbs to the gate at the top right-hand corner of the field. Turn right along a green track which passes Caerberllan farm to come to the road. Turn right, go left at the crossroads and cross Pont Ystumanner (a bridge).

6 On the other side, a footpath signpost highlights a track on the left, which passes below Rhiwlas farm and continues as a green path above the river. The path eases across the slopes of Gamallt and swings left with the valley.

7 Beyond a river gorge, the path approaches the back of Abergynolwyn village and turns left to cross an old iron bridge across the river. Turn right along an unsurfaced street to return to the village centre.

walk information

➤ **DISTANCE**	5 miles (8km)
➤ **MINIMUM TIME**	3hrs
➤ **ASCENT/GRADIENT**	656ft (200m) ▲▲▲
➤ **LEVEL OF DIFFICULTY**	👬👬👬
➤ **PATHS**	Field paths and tracks, 14 stiles
➤ **LANDSCAPE**	Pastured hills and valleys
➤ **SUGGESTED MAPS**	OS Explorer OL23 Cadair Idris & Llyn Tegid
➤ **START/FINISH**	Grid reference: SH 677069
➤ **DOG FRIENDLINESS**	Dogs should be on leads at all times
➤ **PARKING**	Car park by community centre in Abergynolwyn
➤ **PUBLIC TOILETS**	At community centre

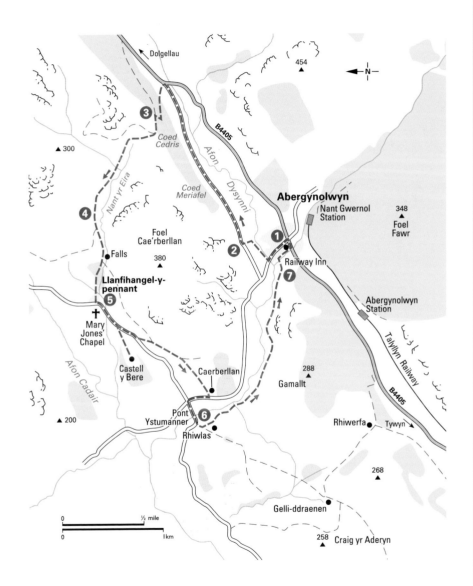

Follow in the footsteps of monks, martyrs and merchants, and through more than 1,500 years of history, both clerical and industrial.

How Grey was my Valley

ABOVE: A pedestrianised street in Holywell town centre
LEFT: The 15th-century St Winefride's Chapel in Holywell

A good head of water has served the Greenfield Valley well over the centuries gushing out from a spring on the limestone hillsides beneath Holywell. Geologists call this a natural phenomenon, but romantics say St Winefride's Well dates back to the 7th century after St Beuno set up a church here. His daughter Winefride taught in the convent and caught the eye of Caradog, the local chieftain. After being spurned by the young nun, the vengeful Caradog drew his sword and cut off her head; a spring emerged where her head hit the ground. Since then, pilgrims have been coming to this 'Lourdes of Wales' to take the healing waters.

Basingwerk Abbey

Religious connections also played a prominent role here in the 12th century, when the Savignac Order, which was later to be combined with the Cistercians, set up Basingwerk Abbey at the bottom of the hill. The abbey is the first thing you see at the start of the walk and, although it has been in ruins since the Dissolution of the Monasteries, a couple of fine sandstone arches remain in good condition.

The Industrial Revolution

The monks were the first to utilise the power of the stream when they built a corn mill here. It would be one of many industrial buildings that would later occupy the whole valley from the mid-17th century onwards. Tall brick chimneys, mill pools, reservoirs and waterwheels sprung up everywhere, and steam from those chimneys billowed up through the trees as the valley was put to work. Thomas Williams of the Parys Mine Company established a rolling mill and the Abbey Wire Mill here, while in the Battery Works up the hill the workforce hammered out brass pots and pans that were used for the slave trade. Ships would leave Liverpool laden with brassware for West Africa, where they would load up with slaves for the Caribbean, returning to Liverpool with sugar, tobacco and cotton. In 1869 the railway came and by 1912 a full passenger service was operating from Greenfield to Holywell. At a gradient of 1 in 27 it became the steepest conventional passenger railway in Great Britain, and continued to be so until its closure in 1954. One by one the mills shut down. Some were demolished, others were left to crumble just like the abbey they surrounded.

Heritage Park

Today the valley is a heritage park and relics of the old industries sit among pleasant gardens. The Greenfield Valley makes a wonderful walk through more than 1,500 years of history and, as you cross the high fields later in this walk, you can see the new century's industries along the coastline of the Dee Estuary far below.

walk directions

1 Take the footpath that emerges from the back of the car park on the left-hand side and follow it around the abbey.

2 Turn left between the visitor centre and the old schoolhouse on a track that passes Abbey Farm. Take the left fork by the brick walls of Abbey Wire Mill, following the sign to the Fishing Pool, a lily covered pond.

3 Beyond Victoria Mill take the lower right-hand fork then bear right past some fixed iron gates to pass the crumbling remains of Meadow Mill. Beyond the mill turn left up some steps, climbing up by a weir and back on to the main track.

4 Turn right along the lower track, eventually passing above Hall's soft drinks factory. Beyond a brick chimney, fork off right down to a kissing gate and wind out to the road. Turn left along the road as far as St Winefride's Chapel and Well. When you've viewed these, go back down the road to the Royal Oak Inn.

5 Climb the lane, called Green Bank, that begins from the opposite side of the road. Beyond the houses bear off right along a waymarked track. Keep ahead past the entrance to a small housing estate on a sunken hedged path. Enter a field over a stile at the top.

6 Head out to the distant right corner and continue at the edge of the next field. Maintain your north-westerly direction to a stile and keep going to another, part-way down the boundary. Walk on with a hedge on your right, exiting over a stile onto a track.

7 Leave the cart track where it swings round to the right for a second time and follow a signed footpath across a meadow and then through trees to the banks of Afon Marsiandwr. After crossing the stream the path climbs out of the woods and crosses a field to a country lane.

8 Turn right along the lane following it down to reach the coast road (A548). Cross the busy road with care. The continuing footpath to the seashore lies immediately opposite you, over a step stile. Cross a field and then a railway track, again with care as trains are not infrequent, and continue walking until you get to the inner flood embankments where you turn right.

9 The footpath comes out by Greenfield Dock. Turn right here along the lane back into Greenfield. Turn left to return to the car park.

walk information

➤ **DISTANCE**	5 miles (8km)
➤ **MINIMUM TIME**	3hrs
➤ **ASCENT/GRADIENT**	558ft (170m)
➤ **LEVEL OF DIFFICULTY**	
➤ **PATHS**	Woodland paths and tracks, lanes, field paths and coastal embankment, 9 stiles
➤ **LANDSCAPE**	Wooded former industrial valley, pastured hillside and coast
➤ **SUGGESTED MAPS**	OS Explorer 265 Clwydian Range
➤ **START/FINISH**	Grid reference: SJ 197775
➤ **DOG FRIENDLINESS**	Dogs should be on lead
➤ **PARKING**	Just off A548 at Greenfield
➤ **PUBLIC TOILETS**	By visitor centre

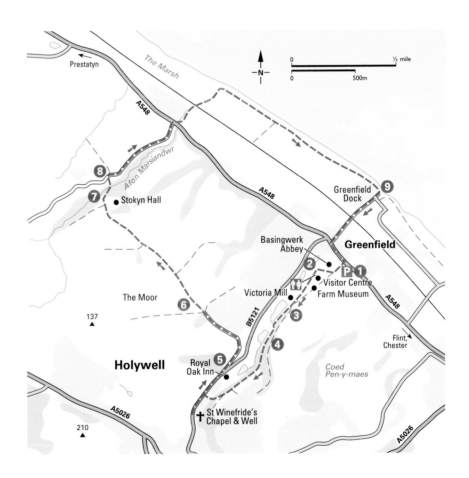

Visit an Iron Age fort and look down on
the magnificent land- and seascapes that
inspired a 19th-century priest and poet.

With the Poet to Mynydd y Gaer

ABOVE: The remote Sychnant Chapel stands
in its churchyard
LEFT: The village of Llannefydd surrounded by fields

The 19th-century poet and Jesuit priest, Gerard Manley Hopkins (1844–89) loved the borderlands of Clwyd. He came to St Beuno's College in the nearby Clwydian Hills in 1874 to study theology. Here he learned the native tongue and applied the rhythms of Welsh poetry to his own religious works, inventing what he described as 'sprung rhythm'. Unfortunately, he was never published in his own lifetime and it was only in 1918, when friend Robert Bridges became Poet Laureate and sent Hopkins' poems to a publisher, that they saw the light of day.

The Village

This short walk will take you from the peaceful little village of Llannefydd and over one of Clwyd's little hills, where you can view the length of Hopkins' Elwy Valley. Llannefydd is 800ft (244m) above sea level and was named after the 5th-century Celtic Saint, Nefydd, who established her church near the spot where the present 13th-century church stands. Before the great engineer Thomas Telford built his A5 trunk road in the 1820s, Llannefydd was on the main route to Holyhead, and the Hawk & Buckle Inn was a stop-off for the stagecoaches. Today Llannefydd is a peaceful backwater and non-the-worse for that – it will be our discovery!

The Fort

Mynydd y Gaer above the village is an Iron Age encampment, probably about 3,000 years old. The ancient earthwork ramparts around its outer edge are well preserved, though today they're covered with scrub and gorse. At the top of the hill there's a more modern cairn – a pile of stones with a pole in the middle. From here you can see why those early settlers chose this place – they could see for miles across the land and out to sea! Below and to the north you can view Gerard Manley Hopkins' beloved Afon Elwy, twisting and turning between low wooded hills. It meanders into the beautiful flatlands of the Vale of Clwyd before finally flowing into the sea at Rhyl, whose tall white tower can be easily picked out against the bay. On either side you can see a mountain range. To the east the heathered Clwydians, which decline to the sea at Prestatyn, and to the west are the distinctive Snowdonian peaks, from the Carneddau whalebacks in the north to Snowdon itself.

Eyecatching Light

Strangely enough, if the sun shines it may well be a little reservoir, Plâs-uchaf, that catches your eye. Beautifully set tucked beneath Mynydd y Gaer's west slopes, its surrounding velvety pastures, complete with whitewashed farmhouse, make it stand out as an idyllic retreat. You get a closer look on the way back on a lovely green track that skirts the foot of the hill and its northern shores.

ABOVE: The Ogwr Fach valley

walk directions

1. Turn left out of the car park and follow the lane signposted to Llanfair TH (the TH standing for Talhaiarn). Where a road comes in from the left, go though a gate on the right-hand side and traverse the fields with a hedge and fence on your left.

2. Beyond a gate in the far corner, turn left with the hedge, continuing uphill in a second field and then over a stile. Leave through a gate at the top, winding out of a small enclosure onto a lane by Ochor-y-gaer. Turn left.

3. Where the road turns sharply to the left, leave it and double-back to the right on a tarmac track climbing up to Bryn Hwylfa. Just past the whitewashed cottage, turn left along an enclosed grass track climbing the hill. Beyond a gate a grassy footpath winds through gorse and

walk information

➤ **DISTANCE**	3.25 miles (5.2km)
➤ **MINIMUM TIME**	2hrs
➤ **ASCENT/GRADIENT**	656ft (200m) ▲▲▲
➤ **LEVEL OF DIFFICULTY**	👤👤👤
➤ **PATHS**	Field paths and tracks, 1 stile
➤ **LANDSCAPE**	Pastured hills
➤ **SUGGESTED MAPS**	OS Explorer 264 Vale of Clwyd
➤ **START/FINISH**	Grid reference: SH 981706
➤ **DOG FRIENDLINESS**	Farmland – dogs should be on lead at all times
➤ **PARKING**	Llannefydd village car park
➤ **PUBLIC TOILETS**	At car park

scrub before veering left beneath the outer ring defences of the Iron Age fort.

4 Where the gorse bushes become more sparse, climb right to reach the brow of the hill. Go through a farm gate to reach the cairn at the summit. Descend north from here, to pick up a track that passes a hilltop farm, Ty-newydd, before descending left to meet another lane.

5 Turn left along the lane, but leave it at a right-hand bend for a grass track continuing ahead to pass above the shores of Plâs-uchaf Reservoir. Past the lake, the track swings left towards Sychnant.

6 Beyond a gate the track becomes a path, winding through woodland before coming to the lane that you left on your outward route. Turn right along the lane then first left, heading straight back to Llannefydd.

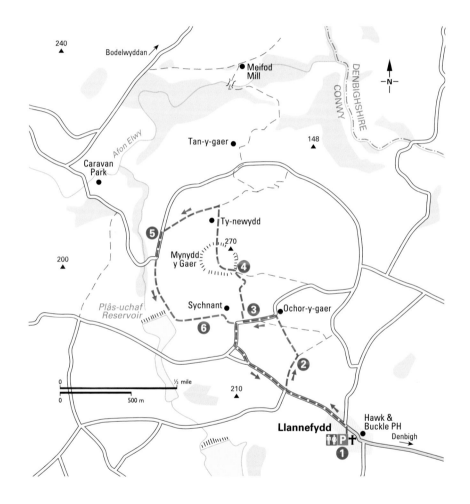

Walk to the highest of the Clwydian Hills and see a beautiful wooded limestone valley on the way.

Moel Famau: the Mother Mountain

ABOVE: *Jubilee Tower stands at the top of Moel Famau*
LEFT: *Sunset adds a touch of gold to the Vale of Clwyd*

If you're driving into Wales from the north-west, the chances are that the first hills you'll see are the Clwydians, dark rolling ridges that rise up from the sea at Prestatyn and decline 20 miles (32km) or so south in the fields of the Alun Valley. Although the hills are empty these days, at one time they were highly populated. Climb to the tops and you'll see Iron and Bronze Age forts scattered about the hilltops, some of them among the best preserved in Wales.

At Loggerheads

One of the best places to start a walk in the Clwydians is Loggerheads. The path from the information centre follows the shallow, swift-flowing River Alun through a narrow limestone valley filled with wych elm and oak. In July, you'll see limestone flora, including field scabious, wild thyme, rock rose and bloody cranesbill, while above there are spotted woodpeckers, tawny owls and nuthatches.

On the Top

The climb out of the valley includes a short traverse of farmland before clambering through heather fields to Moel Famau, which means 'mother mountain' and at 1,818ft (554m) is the highest of the range. The monument on the summit was built in 1810 to celebrate the jubilee of King George III. Its square tower and spire were wrecked by a violent gale some 50 years later, and the place lay in ruins until 1970 when it was tidied up. Below and to the west there's the much older site of Moel y Gaer, one of those fascinating hill-forts with concentric earthwork rings sculpted into a grassy knoll. Casting your eyes beyond the rings and across the green fields and chequered hedgerows of the Vale of Clwyd, it's interesting to pick out the familiar skyline summits of Snowdonia. Tryfan's jagged crest is easy to spot, but somehow you cannot quite see Snowdon and that's because Moel Siabod, prima donna that it feels it is, has elbowed its way to the front, to hide the real star of the show, Snowdon, and confuse the issue. Fortunately there are topographs to help you out.

The ridge walking from the summit is delightful. A wide path takes you down to the forest, where it continues down a grassy ride. While the spruce trees are not an attractive habitat for a wide range of species you might easily spot a song thrush, colourful chaffinches or coal tits; or maybe, just maybe, a sparrowhawk. Country lanes and farm pastures take you down to the banks of the River Alun which guides you back to Loggerheads.

walk directions

1 Go past the front of the Loggerheads Country Park Information Centre, café and other buildings, cross the bridge over the Alun and turn left along the surfaced path through the valley. Keep to the main, near-level path, marked the Leete Path.

2 Pass the A.L.Y.N. Kennels, cross a lane, then look out for a small, often slippery path on the left (signed Moel Famau). This leads to a footbridge. Across this the path heads west, then staggers to the right across a farm lane and climbs past a farmhouse. Enclosed by thickets, it climbs to the right of another house to reach a T-junction of country lanes. Go straight ahead and follow the lane uphill, then turn right to follow the track that passes Ffrith farm before swinging left to climb round the pastured slopes of Ffrith Mountain. Take the left fork in the tracks (at grid ref 177637).

3 The route skirts a spruce plantation and climbs to a crossroads of tracks, marked by a tall waymarker post. Turn left here on a wide path over undulating heather slopes towards the tower on the top of Moel Famau.

4 From the summit, head south-east and go through a gate at the end of the wall to follow a wide track, marked with red-tipped waymarker posts, south-east along the forest's edge. The track continues its descent through the trees to meet the roadside car park/picnic area 0.75 mile (1.2km) east of Bwlch Penbarra's summit (See Information Panel on using shuttle bus).

5 Turn left along the road, before turning right when you get to the first junction. The quiet lane leads to the busy A494. Cross the main road with care and continue along the hedge-lined lane staggered to the right.

6 A waymarked path on the left heads north-east across fields towards the banks of the Alun. Don't cross the river at the bridge, but head north, through the gateway and across more fields, passing a stone-built house below on the right. Turn right on the A494. It's just 0.5 mile (800m) from here to the Loggerheads Country Park entrance, and there are verges and paths to walk on.

walk information

➤ **DISTANCE**	8 miles (12.9km)
➤ **MINIMUM TIME**	4hrs 30min
➤ **ASCENT/GRADIENT**	1,608ft (490m) ▲▲▲
➤ **LEVEL OF DIFFICULTY**	👥👥👥
➤ **PATHS**	Well-defined paths and forestry tracks, 8 stiles
➤ **LANDSCAPE**	Heather moor, forest and farmland
➤ **SUGGESTED MAPS**	OS Explorer 265 Clwydian Range
➤ **START/FINISH**	Grid reference: SJ 198625
➤ **DOG FRIENDLINESS**	Dogs could run free in forest and on heather ridges
➤ **PARKING**	Pay car park by Loggerheads Country Park Visitor Centre
➤ **PUBLIC TOILETS**	At Visitor Centre
➤ **NOTE**	Route can be shortened by taking regular Moel Famau shuttle bus, which runs on Sundays (July to September) and bank holidays, from forestry car park to Loggerheads

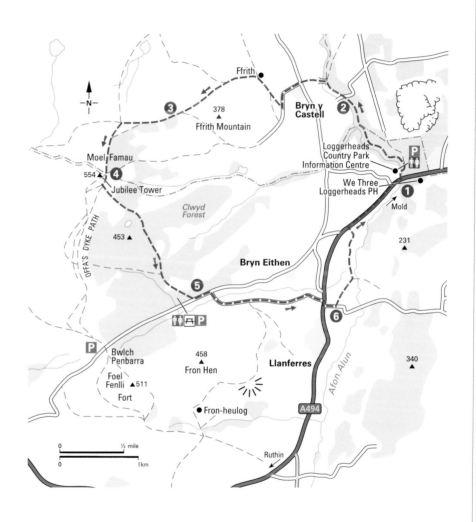

Climbing above Bala to get the best view of Wales' largest natural lake.

A View of Bala's Lake – Llyn Tegid

ABOVE: *Bala Lake miniature railway*
LEFT: *Sailors enjoy all that George Borrow's 'Lake of Beauty' has to offer*

'It was a beautiful evening… the wind was blowing from the south, and tiny waves were beating against the shore, which consisted of small brown pebbles. The lake has certainly not its name, which signifies Lake of Beauty, for nothing'
George Borrow, Wild Wales, 1862

Borrow had been staying at the White Lion in Bala and had been impressed with the place and its people. Bala is an austere town, close to the banks of two great rivers, the Tryweryn and the Dee, and the shore of Wales' largest natural lake, Llyn Tegid.

Religion and Wool

The town's many chapels give a hint to its religious roots. You'll see the statue of Dr Lewis Edwards, founder of the Methodist College, and, opposite the White Lion, one of the Revd Thomas Charles, a founder of the British and Foreign Bible Society. Bala's employment was based around the woollen industry, and the town was noted for its stockings. Thomas Pennant came here in 1786 and painted a fascinating picture of life in the town: 'Round the place, women and children are in full employ, knitting along the roads; and mixed with them Herculean figures appear, assisting their omphales in this effeminate employ.'

Recreational Activities

Llyn Tegid is every bit as beautiful as Borrow suggests and it's popular for watersports. When the south-westerlies blow, Bala has waves like an angry ocean. It's favoured by anglers too. Pike, perch, trout, salmon and roach are plentiful, but the fish Llyn Tegid is famous for is the Gwyniad, which is not unlike a freshwater herring. It is said these fish were trapped here after the last ice age. You come to the old Norman motte-and-bailey castle of Tomen y Mur soon after turning your back on the lake. Some say that the mound goes back to Roman times, but it is known that the castle was captured from the Normans by Llewelyn ap Iowerth in 1202. One of those Welsh steam railways has its terminus right next to the old castle site and it's fascinating to see the old steam engines puffing along the lakeside. However, we are in search of higher things, so climb through woods and upland fields until you get your view. From up high you can see Tegid's blue waters, seemingly perfect and still from this distance, and stretching 4.5 miles (7.2km) along its rift valley towards Dolgellau. White farmhouses are dotted on pleasant pastured hills. The Dee, so wide down river from Bala, has anonymous beginnings in the peat bogs beneath Dduallt, whose dark crags rise high on the north-west horizon. It's time to descend, through more oak woods, and further, beneath western hemlock and larch, finally to reach the lakeshores and the welcome comforts of the town.

RIGHT: The Bala Lake Railway uses a 2ft narrow gauge steam train

walk directions

1 Go to the north corner of the car park in Bala to access the riverside path. Turn right to follow a raised embankment along the west bank of the Tryweryn. After a dog-leg to the right, passing through two kissing gates, the footpath continues, first by the banks of the Tryweryn, then by the north banks of the Dee.

2 On reaching the road, cross the bridge over the River Dee, then a smaller, older bridge. Go through a kissing gate to cross a small field to Bala Station on Bala Lake Railway. A footbridge allows you to cross the track before traversing two small fields.

3 Turn right along a cart track, and continue to pass behind the Bala Lake Hotel. A waymarker points the direction up a grassy bank on the left, and the path continues to a stile and then follows a fence on the right.

4 Descend slightly to cross a stream beside a small cottage, go up again then along a level fence to a stile. Bear left up through some bracken and wind up steeply at first, then continue more easily to a tarmac lane.

5 Turn left along the lane to a cattle grid from where you continue on a stony track, passing through felled plantations.

6 Just before the isolated house of Cefn-ddwygraig, turn left off the track to a ladder stile. Follow a grooved grass track across gorse-covered slopes. Keep left at a fork and then drop down to a stile. The well-waymarked path continues north, with Bala town ahead.

7 Go over a partially hidden step stile into the commercial forestry plantations of Coed Pen-y-bont. A narrow footpath descends to the bottom edge of the woods (ignore the forestry track you meet on the way down).

8 At the bottom of the woods turn right along a track that reaches the road by the Pen-y-Bont Campsite. Turn left along the road, cross the Dee again, bear left and then follow the lakeside footpath past the information centre. When you reach the main road, turn right to explore the fascinating town centre.

LEFT: *Spectators watch the watersports on the scenic Llyn Tegid*

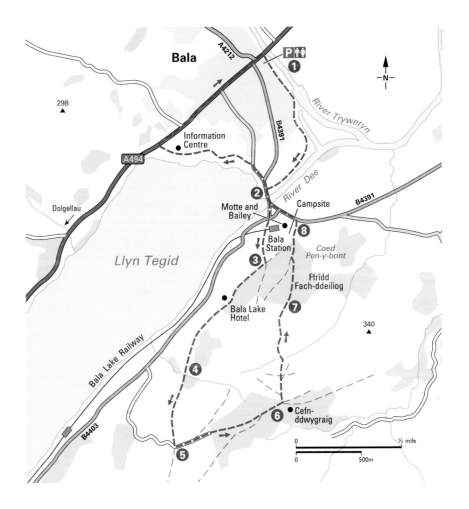

walk information

➤ **DISTANCE**	5 miles (8km)
➤ **MINIMUM TIME**	3hrs
➤ **ASCENT/GRADIENT**	656ft (200m) ▲▲
➤ **LEVEL OF DIFFICULTY**	👤👤👤
➤ **PATHS**	Woodland and field paths, 7 stiles
➤ **LANDSCAPE**	Woods and upland pasture
➤ **SUGGESTED MAPS**	OS Explorer OL23 Cadair Idris & Llyn Tegid, or OS Explorer OL18 Harlech, Porthmadog and Bala
➤ **START/FINISH**	Grid reference: SH 929361
➤ **DOG FRIENDLINESS**	Dogs should be on lead at all times
➤ **PARKING**	Car park at entrance to Bala town from east
➤ **PUBLIC TOILETS**	At car park

*Discover an earthly heaven in one
of ancient Clwyd's truly green and
pleasant valleys.*

In the Beautiful Ceiriog Valley

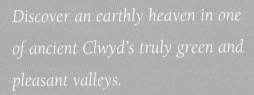

*ABOVE: One of the pretty village gardens in
Llanarmon Dyffryn Ceiriog
LEFT: Llanarmon Dyffryn Ceiriog's name is
derived from the 5th Century missionary,
St Garmon*

David Lloyd George, the last Liberal Party Prime Minister of Britain, described the Ceiriog Valley as 'a piece of heaven that has fallen to earth'. For 18 miles (29km), from its source on the slopes of Mount Fferna in the Berwyns to its meeting with the Dee, the beautiful Afon Ceiriog meanders through oak woods, rocky hillsides and fertile cattle pastures. Yet in 1923 city planners wanted to turn this little piece of heaven into a huge reservoir. If these planners had won the day, the locals living within an area of 13,600 acres (5,508ha) would have been evicted from their homes. Fortunately Parliament denied their whims.

St Garmon

While Glyn Ceiriog is the largest village, Llanarmon Dyffryn Ceiriog is the most beautiful. Lying by the confluence of the Ceiriog and a tributary, the Gwrachen, it was a natural fording place for drovers bound for the markets of England. You'll be using some of their old roads on this walk. The village and its church take their name from the 5th-century missionary, St Garmon. The present church is early Victorian and, unusually, has two pulpits. A mound in the churchyard, known as Tomen Garmon, is believed to be a Bronze Age burial mound and the place where the missionary preached.

A Pastoral Idyll

The walk begins behind the church, and follows pretty pastures above the Ceiriog and woods full of bluebells before coming to the old Mill (Y Felin) at Tregeiriog. In the 19th century, author George Borrow revelled in the pastoral nature of this landscape. He spent hours standing on the bridge, watching pigs foraging by the river bank while the old Mill's waterwheel slowly turned; a scene he said that 'was well-suited to the brushes of two or three of the old Dutch painters'.

From the old Mill the route climbs on one of those drovers' roads on to the small hills overlooking the valley. You can see many a mile of rolling green hills as a winding green track climbs towards some crags on the horizon. Here you enter a wilder world of rushy moorland with views down the valleys of Nant y Glôg and the Gwrachen. After tramping through the bracken of the high hillside you join another green road which accompanies the Gwrachen. By now you may be following the footsteps of Owain Glyndwr, 15th-century Prince of Wales, who would have passed through Llanarmon when travelling between his residences at Sycharth and Glyndyfrdwy in the Dee Valley.

walk directions

1 From The Hand, take the eastbound lane past the church and uphill with a conifer plantation on the right and the pastures of the Ceiriog below left.

2 At the far end of the plantation leave the road for a farm track on the left. This ends at a barn. Keep to the right of the barn and aim for a gate beyond it. Through the gate maintain your direction, over the shoulder of a grassy knoll, then aim for a stile in a fence ahead. Beyond this, cross another field down to a gate, through which mount a stile on the right.

3 Bear left, crossing two streamlets to join a track past Ty'n-y-fedw farm. Don't go through the gate, but follow a grass path right beside the fence, shortly entering a wood

4 Keep ahead to the far end of the woods. Emerging into a field, a grass trod curves round to a gate at the top corner. Turn right along a rising farm track, ignoring junctions to reach a lane. Next cross to the ongoing track opposite, which climbs on through the high pastures.

5 At a crossroads, turn right along a green track – part of the Upper Ceiriog Way. This heads south-west towards the green hill known as Cefn-Hîr-fynydd.

6 After about 300yds (274m) leave this track through a gate on the right. If you head west by the right edge of the rushy area and towards Pen y Glôg's sparse crags, it will be easy to find the small stile in the next fence, then the wooden gate on the left soon afterwards. Through the gate head downhill with a faint sheep path past a low clump of rocks on the left, and aiming for the distant farm of Cyrchynan-isaf.

7 Lower down, a developing grassy track runs on through the valley of Nant y Glôg contouring the lower slopes of Pen y Glôg, and eventually reaching a gate.

8 After swinging right with the lively stream the track terminates by a lane to the south of Llanarmon Dyffryn Ceiriog. Follow the lane past several attractive cottages and the village school to arrive by the Hand hotel in the village square.

walk information

➤ **DISTANCE**	3.75 miles (6km)
➤ **MINIMUM TIME**	2hrs 30min
➤ **ASCENT/GRADIENT**	853ft (260m) ▲▲▲
➤ **LEVEL OF DIFFICULTY**	🚶🚶🚶
➤ **PATHS**	Sketchy paths and farm tracks, 4 stiles
➤ **LANDSCAPE**	Pastoral hillscapes and river scenery
➤ **SUGGESTED MAPS**	OS Explorer 255 Llangollen & Berwyn
➤ **START/FINISH**	Grid reference: SJ 157328
➤ **DOG FRIENDLINESS**	Whole walk through sheep country, keep dogs on lead
➤ **PARKING**	Roadside parking in village
➤ **PUBLIC TOILETS**	At village hall

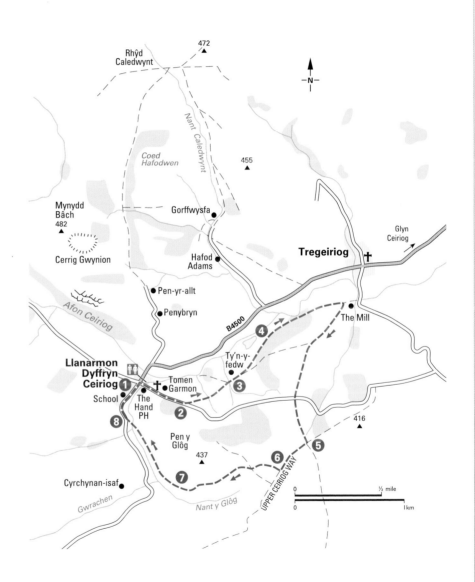

A demanding, but short walk brings magnificent views and a visit to spectacular falls.

Cadair Berwyn and Pistyll Rhaeadr

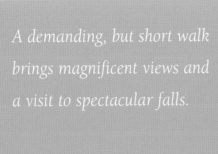

'What shall I liken it to? I scarcely know, unless to an immense skein of silk agitated and disturbed by tempestuous blasts, or to the long tail of a grey courser at furious speed'.

This is how author, George Borrow saw the falls of Pistyll Rhaeadr in his travels in *Wild Wales* (1862). The mountain valley, fringed by crag and dappled with heather and bracken, leads to Llyn Lluncaws. Here's a dramatic scene – a wild Welsh cwm in which the lake lies dark and sombre among frazzled heather that can't quite take hold and tussocky moor grass that fills in the extra spaces.

ABOVE: Pistyll Rhaeadr, Wales's tallest waterfall tumbles 240 feet from the Berwyn Mountains
LEFT: Purple foxgloves on the side of a wooded valley near Pistyll Rhaeadr

Up in the Gods

A peat and slate path beats a tortuous route by the cwm's cliff edge up on to the ridge, and you discover why you came up here in the first place. You find yourself up in the gods, looking over a stage where there's a cast of thousands. At the front, the green cloaked Dee Valley weaves its way though the heather hills of Llangollen and the jagged Aran mountains towards the chorus line, where Cadair Idris, the Rhinogs, and Snowdon parade themselves aloof and often with their heads in the clouds. In the alternative theatre at your back, the Tanat Valley scenery of fields and hedges gives way to the little blue hills of Cheshire and Shropshire in England.

The Berwyns are one of the few places in Wales where the cloudberry grows. These shrubs, not unlike a bramble but lacking thorns, cling closely to the ground. You'll have to be up early to get to the sparse fruits first. They belong to the blackberry family but are orange and taste like raspberries.

Cadair Berwyn

At one time everybody assumed that Moel Sych and Cadair Berwyn were, at 2,713ft (827m), jointly the highest Berwyns – the OS maps that walkers used said so. But everyone who walked the Berwyns looked quizzically across to that little rock peak forming Cadair Berwyn's south summit – it seemed higher. When the OS checked their large scale maps they found that, at 2,723ft (830m), it indeed was the 'tops'.

No Warning

Moel Sych is just a broad flat top, with a cairn for you to pat on your way down to the falls. Amid pretty mixed woodland the peaceful Afon Disgynfa trickles playfully over rocks then, without warning, tumbles off the end of the world. Walkers who have made the ascent look on, amazed, then take the gentler zig-zag route down to the same place. Back in Tan-y-pistyll the café awaits!

1. From the more easterly, and the smaller, of the two car parks turn right along the road for about 400yds (366m), then turn sharp left to follow a wide grassy track that climbs north-west to enter the cwm of Nant y Llyn. At an obvious fork keep right on a rising track heading north towards the crags of Cerrig Poethion.

2. The track degenerates into a path that traverses hillsides scattered with gorse. Higher up it crosses two streams before reaching Llyn Lluncaws in the moss and heather cwm. Now the path climbs south of the lake and up a shale and grass spur to the left of Moel Sych's crags. Follow the path along the edge of the crags on the right to reach the col between Moel Sych and Cadair Berwyn. From here climb to the rocky south top of the latter peak. The onward trip to the trig point on Cadair Berwyn's lower north summit is straightforward but offers no advantages as a viewpoint.

3. From the south top retrace your footsteps to the col, but this time instead of tracing the cliff edge you now follow the ridge fence to the cairn on Moel Sych summit plateau, crossing a stile just before reaching it.

4. Recross the stile and turn right (south) to follow the fence down a wide, peaty spur cloaked with moor grass, mosses and a little heather. Over a slight rise, the path descends again to a stile (wobbly when checked) before dropping into the high moorland cwm of the Disgynfa, where the path is met by a stony track that climbs from the base of the falls.

walk information

➤ **DISTANCE**	5 miles (8km)
➤ **MINIMUM TIME**	3hrs
➤ **ASCENT/GRADIENT**	1,870ft (570m) ▲▲▲
➤ **LEVEL OF DIFFICULTY**	🅰🅰🅰🅰
➤ **PATHS**	Well-defined paths and tracks, 7 stiles
➤ **LANDSCAPE**	Mountain and moorland
➤ **SUGGESTED MAPS**	OS Explorer 255 Llangollen & Berwyn
➤ **START/FINISH**	Grid reference: SJ 076293
➤ **DOG FRIENDLINESS**	Sheep usually present: dogs should be on lead
➤ **PARKING**	Car park 220yds (201m) before Tan-y-pistyll farm/café, where there's another pay car park
➤ **PUBLIC TOILETS**	At Tan-y-pistyll pay car park

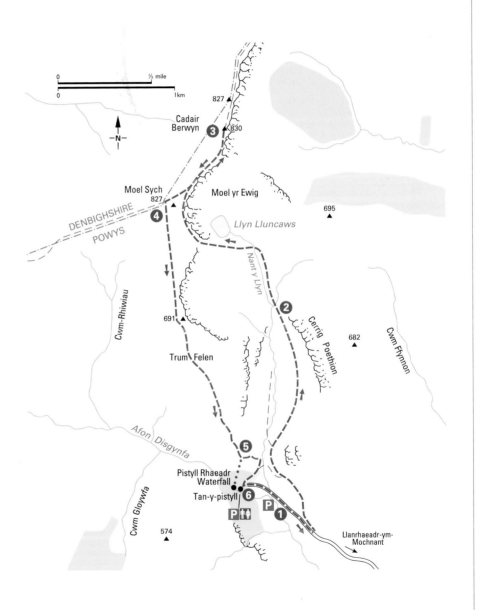

5 If you want to make a there-and-back detour to the top of the falls, ignore the stony track, and instead go through a gate into the forest and follow the path to the river. If not, descend along the previously mentioned track, which zigzags down before turning right to head for the Tan-y-pistyll complex. There's a path to the bottom of the falls starting from the café. It leads to a footbridge across the Afon Rhaeadr for the best views.

6 From the café it's a short walk along the road to the car park.

From the Dee to the Eglwyseg,
this walk discovers a fascinating
tapestry of history and landscape.

Idyllic Valle Crucis and Dinas Bran

The River Dee is never more attractive than in the Vale of Llangollen where it meanders around small but shapely hills, through forest and field, and beneath terraces of limestone. Llangollen town has prospered with all this beauty, and today is a bustling holiday resort based on an impressive five-arched bridge over the Dee – one of the seven wonders of Wales. Watching over the town there's a mysterious ruined castle, Dinas Bran, the fort of the crows.

ABOVE: *Ruins of Castle Dinas Bran*
at Llangollen
LEFT: *The western front and elaborate carved*
doorways of Valle Crucis Abbey dominate these
13th-century ruins

Strolling by the Canal

This walk explores the countryside around the town and starts with a stroll along the canal. Colourful barges, some horse drawn, still cruise down the waters where there are swans and hungry ducks to persuade you to share your sandwiches. When it's time to leave them behind you enter the little valley of the Eglwyseg.

The Abbey

A short distance along this valley, the walk comes to the ruined abbey of Valle Crucis, a name that means simply valley of the cross. The cross concerned used to be on top of the Pillar of Eliseg, now sadly a rather degraded roadside relic, but once an elegant memorial to Eliseg, a ninth-century Prince of Powys. Established in 1201 by Cistercian monks from Strata Marcella near Welshpool, Valle Crucis Abbey was beautifully sited in fertile pastures, where the monks could grow crops and tend sheep. A modern caravan site has been sited next to the ruins, but the abbey is still impressive, with many original features surviving the ravages of time and the Reformation. The chapter house still has its impressive rib-vaulted roof, the windows of the east wall still reflect perfectly in the monks' fish pond, and the west front still boasts an elaborate carved doorway and a beautiful rose window.

Climbing to the Fort of the Crows

The walk climbs out of the valley to a little country lane, which takes you alongside the foot of Creigiau Eglwyseg, as fine a parade of tiered limestone crags as you'll see in any Yorkshire dale. But the best comes last, for facing those crags is Dinas Bran, that shapely hill with the fort on top. When you get to the top, the ruins are large and impressive. Unlike Conwy, Harlech and Caernarfon, this is a true Welsh castle, probably built for those same indigenous Princes of Powys. Built on the strategic site of an existing Iron Age fort – you can still see the old embankment – the castle never played a major role in battle. Its exact demise is unknown, but historians believe that the Welsh occupiers fled before the troops of Edward I laid it to waste. It's a fine viewpoint too. The fields of Eglwyseg seem to have a green velvet quality, framed to perfection by those limestone crags, and there's a bird's-eye view of Llangollen.

RIGHT: A view across the valley from Castell Dinas

walk directions

1　Walk from the car park to the main street and go left over Llangollen Bridge. Turn right and then left, climbing to the canal and dropping on to the tow path by the café.

2　After about a mile (1.6km) the canal veers left. Leave the tow path to cross the canal on an ivy-clad bridge. Turn right along the pavement of the main road (A542). Cross the road and take a farm track signed 'FP to Valle Crucis'. The track heads north past the old abbey, where the track ends. A footpath continues, along the left edge of a field.

3　After crossing the stile at Abbey Cottage turn right for a few paces, then left to follow a well-defined track through woodland. When you get to Hendre farm take the right-hand fork leading to a narrow lane at Tan-y-Fron.

4　Turn right along the road, heading towards the prominent cliffs of Eglwyseg, then right again, along the lane that hugs the foot of the cliffs.

5　After 0.25 mile (400m), leave through the second of adjacent gates on the right. Walk away beside successive fields, crossing a stile by farm sheds on to a track back through to the lane. Go right past a junction.

6　When you reach the second junction take the right-hand fork for a few paces, then go through the gate on the right, on to a waymarked footpath leading to Castell Dinas Bran. From the crumbling west walls of the castle descend on a zig-zag path. Go around the right-hand side of a little knoll at the bottom of the hill to join a track near a house called Tirionfa.

LEFT: The 13th-century ruins of Valle Crucis Abbey

7 At a junction, keep ahead to a second cottage, there crossing a stile into a field. Trace the left-hand edge of the field down to a narrow lane.

8 Across this, the route continues along a contained path, passing a school before crossing a road and then the Llangollen Canal close to the start of the walk. Descend the road down to Llangollen Bridge before crossing back into the car park.

walk information

➤ **DISTANCE**	6.75 miles (10.9km)
➤ **MINIMUM TIME**	4hrs
➤ **ASCENT/GRADIENT**	1,296ft (395m)
➤ **LEVEL OF DIFFICULTY**	
➤ **PATHS**	Tow path, farm tracks and field paths, 5 stiles
➤ **LANDSCAPE**	Pastoral and wooded hillsides with limestone scenery
➤ **SUGGESTED MAPS**	OS Explorer 255 Llangollen and Berwyn
➤ **START/FINISH**	Grid reference: SJ 214420
➤ **DOG FRIENDLINESS**	On lead on farmland and country lanes. Can run free on canal tow path
➤ **PARKING**	Long-stay car park in East Street, just south-west of the bridge
➤ **PUBLIC TOILETS**	At car park

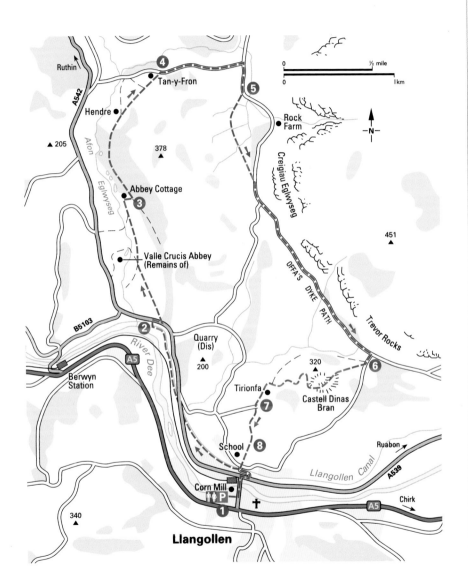

See how the Earls of Powis lived as you walk through their deer park and past their huge red palace on the hill.

Powis Castle and the Montgomery Canal

ABOVE: *The Powys Railway steams through the Welsh countryside at Welshpool*
LEFT: *Powis Castle was home to a dynasty of Welsh princes*

A prosperous and bustling market town set amid rolling green hills, wood and hedgerows, Welshpool has always been synonymous with the River Severn, which flows through it. It was the Severn that brought trade to the town, for it was navigable by boat. The town was, until 1835, known as Pool and some of the old mileposts still refer to Pool. The 'Welsh' was added to distinguish the place from Poole in Dorset.

A Majestic Setting

When you walk up the busy High Street today you'll notice the fine architecture, most of it dating from Georgian times, like the Royal Oak Hotel, but also many older half-timbered buildings. Almost every tourist who comes to Welshpool comes to see the fine castle of Powis. On this route you turn off through the impressive wrought-iron gates before strolling along the long drive through the estate's parklands. Proud oaks are scattered on the well-mown grasslands and a majestic scene is set when you see deer roaming among the trees, maybe antlered stags, or those cute little fallow deer.

Today the castle is a grand red mansion, with castellated ramparts, tall chimneys, rows of fine leaded windows and 17th-century balustraded terraces looking over manicured lawns and neatly clipped yews. Lead statues of a shepherd and shepherdess survive from those early days and keep watch over the colourful shrubs and perennial borders.

Warring Princes

However, the scene would have been so different in 1200, when the castle was first built for the warring Princes of Powys. The battlements would have been there, but there would have been no elegant windows or pretty gardens, for this place was designed to repel enemies, both English and Welsh: more often than not Powis sided with the English, even against the Glyndwr rebellion. The fact that Powis has been continuously occupied has meant that it has made a successful transition from fortress to a comfortable grand mansion.

In 1587 the powerful Herbert family, who became the Earls of Powis, took possession of the castle. They were to reside here until 1988, when the 6th Earl died, and were responsible for the transition. Only for a brief period, when they were attacked by Cromwellian forces and replaced by their bitter rivals, the Myddletons of Chirk, were the Royalist Herberts displaced.

On leaving the castle behind, you are in rural Wales and you descend to the tow path of the Montgomery Canal at the Belan Locks. Built by three different companies and opened in stages from 1796, the canal was designed for narrowboats. Today it is a quiet backwater and a pleasant return route to the wharf at Welshpool.

RIGHT: Colourful flowers at Powis Castle

walk information

➤ **DISTANCE**	4 miles (6.4km)
➤ **MINIMUM TIME**	2hrs
➤ **ASCENT/GRADIENT**	328ft (100m) ▲▲▲
➤ **LEVEL OF DIFFICULTY**	🏃🏃🏃
➤ **PATHS**	Tarmac drive, field path, canal tow path, 3 stiles
➤ **LANDSCAPE**	Country town, parkland and canal
➤ **SUGGESTED MAPS**	OS Explorer 216 Welshpool & Montgomery
➤ **START/FINISH**	Grid reference: SJ 226075
➤ **DOG FRIENDLINESS**	Dogs not allowed on the Powis Castle Estate
➤ **PARKING**	Large pay car park off Church Street, Welshpool
➤ **PUBLIC TOILETS**	By information centre in car park

walk directions

1 From the main car park go past the tourist information centre then go left along Church Street. At the crossroads in the centre of town turn right to head up Broad Street, which later becomes High Street.

2 When you get to a point just beyond the town hall, turn left past a small car parking area and pass through the impressive wrought iron gates of the Powis Castle Estate. Now follow the tarmac drive through the park grounds and past Llyn Du (which means the black lake in English).

3 Take the right fork, the high road, which leads to the north side of the castle. You can detour from the walk here to

visit the world-famous gardens and the castle with its fine paintings and furniture and works of Indian art collected by Robert Clive. Continue on the walk on the high road and follow it past two more pools on the left and the Ladies Pool on the right to reach a country lane.

4 Turn left along the country lane. Opposite the next estate entrance leave the lane over a stile beside a gate on the right, from which a grass track winds down to a bridge. Climb away beside the right-hand fence. Continue over another stile in the corner along an old way, which gently falls to a lane beside the Montgomery Canal. This canal, which runs for 33 miles (53km) from Welsh Frankton in Shropshire to Newtown in Powys, is gradually being restored. You may see a number of narrowboats cruising along this section.

5 Turn over the bridge at Belan Locks, immediately dropping left to the canal tow path. Head north along the canal, later passing beneath the main road. Entering Welshpool, remain on the tow path, passing the Powysland Museum and Montgomery Canal Centre (on the opposite bank), with its exhibits of local agriculture, crafts and the canal and railway systems. Beyond a short aqueduct and former railway bridge, climb out to the road and turn left back to the car park.

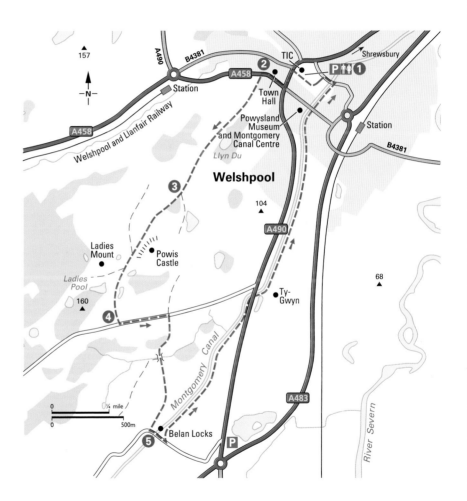

LEFT: Powys Castle atop Ladies Mount near Welshpool

111

Walking in Safety

All these walks are suitable for any reasonably fit person, but less experienced walkers should try the easier walks first. Route finding is usually straightforward, but you will find that an Ordnance Survey map is a useful addition to the route maps and descriptions.

Risks

Although each walk here has been researched with a view to minimising the risks to the walkers who follow its route, no walk in the countryside can be considered to be completely free from risk. Walking in the outdoors will always require a degree of common sense and judgement to ensure that it is as safe as possible.

- Be particularly careful on cliff paths and in upland terrain, where the consequences of a slip can be very serious.
- Remember to check tidal conditions before walking on the seashore.
- Some sections of route are by, or cross, busy roads. Take care and remember traffic is a danger even on minor country lanes.
- Be careful around farmyard machinery and livestock, especially if you have children with you.
- Be aware of the consequences of changes in the weather and check the forecast before you set out. Carry spare clothing and a torch if you are walking in the winter months. Remember the weather can change very quickly at any time of the year, and in moorland and heathland areas, mist and fog can make route finding much harder. Don't set out in these conditions unless you are confident of your navigation skills in poor visibility. In summer remember to take account of the heat and sun; wear a hat and carry spare water.
- On walks away from centres of population you should carry a whistle and survival bag. If you do have an accident requiring the emergency services, make a note of your position as accurately as possible and dial 999.

Acknowledgements

The Automobile Association would like to thank the following photographers, companies and picture libraries for their assistance in the preparation of this book.

Abbreviations for the picture credits are as follows: (t) top; (b) bottom; (l) left; (r) right; (AA) AA World Travel Library.

2/3 AA/S Watkins; 5 AA/D Croucher; 6 AA/N Jenkins; 7bl AA/S Lewis; 7bcl AA/N Jenkins; 7bcr AA/N Jenkins; 7br AA/N Jenkins; 10/11 AA/S Lewis; 12/13 AA/S Watkins; 13 AA/I Burgum; 14/15 AA/S Watkins; 16 AA/G Matthews; 18/19 ; 19 ; 22/23 AA/P Aithie; 23 AA/R Eames; 24/25 AA/P Aithie; 26 AA/R Newton; 28/29 AA/N Jenkins; 29 AA/R Newton; 30/31 AA/S Lewis; 32 AA/N Jenkins; 34/35 AA/S Lewis; 35 AA/G Matthews; 36/37 AA/S Lewis; 38 AA/W Voysey; 40/41 AA; 41 AA/S Watkins; 43 AA/S Watkins; 44/45 AA/S Watkins; 45 AA/C Jones; 46/47 AA/N Jenkins; 48/49 AA/R Eames; 50/51 AA/N Jenkins; 51 AA/N Jenkins; 54/55 AA/H Williams; 55 AA/S Lewis; 58/59 AA/D Croucher; 59 AA/D Croucher; 60/61 AA/D Croucher; 62 AA/D Croucher; 64/65 AA/W Voysey; 65 AA/R Newton; 66/67 AA/W Voysey; 68 AA/W Voysey; 70/71 AA/D Croucher; 71 ; 74/75 AA/I Burgum; 75 AA/I Burgum; 78/79 ; 79 AA/C Molyneux; 80 ; 82/83 ; 83 ; 86/87 AA/N Jenkins; 87 AA/P Aithie; 88/89 AA/P Aithie; 90 AA/N Jenkins; 92/93 AA/R Eames; 93 AA/N Jenkins; 96/97 AA/D Croucher; 97 AA/D Croucher; 100/101 AA/R Newton; 101 AA/N Jenkins; 102/103 AA/N Jenkins; 104 AA/N Jenkins; 106/107 AA/N Jenkins; 107 AA/R Newton; 108/109 AA/N Jenkins; 110 AA

Every effort has been made to trace the copyright holders, and we apologise in advance for any accidental errors. We would be happy to apply the corrections in the following edition of this publication.